Steelworkers

The Last of the Breed

Dennis L. Crider

PublishAmerica
Baltimore

© 2011 by Dennis L. Crider.
All rights reserved. No part of this book may be reproduced, stored in a retrieval system or transmitted in any form or by any means without the prior written permission of the publishers, except by a reviewer who may quote brief passages in a review to be printed in a newspaper, magazine or journal.

First printing

PublishAmerica has allowed this work to remain exactly as the author intended, verbatim, without editorial input.

Hardcover 978-1-4512-6961-1
Softcover 978-1-4512-6962-8
PUBLISHED BY PUBLISHAMERICA, LLLP
www.publishamerica.com
Baltimore

Printed in the United States of America

Table of Contents

Foreword 7

Chapter 1: How We Came to work in the Mills and Factories 9

Chapter 2: Basic Steelmaking from an Integrated Mill 14

Chapter 3: The 80 Inch Hot Strip Mill 19

Chapter 4: 2B.O.F. 2Caster 39

Chapter 5: Fatalities and Injuries 78

Chapter 6: Departments that Closed 86

Chapter 7: Past and Present Employment in the Mills 99

Conclusion 103

Foreword

This book is dedicated to the men and women of America who have worked in the steel mills, factories, and other manufacturing segments of this country who have helped build this country into the great country it is today. Quite often Hollywood and others have downplayed these jobs as unattractive, dirty, dangerous, and not requiring a lot of mentality to perform. This book is dedicated to all of you who have worked these dirty jobs years ago no one wanted but today in this economy people would literally kill for jobs today. From the dock jobs on the coasts, to the construction jobs on the roads and cities, to the automotive plants, to the steel mills, and all the other jobs where we make things to keep this country running smoothly.

Those of you that have worked in grease pits, smelly jobs, heat so hot it takes your breath away, wheel changes on cranes when a hot mill is running beneath you, heat exhaustion where you quit sweating and feel like you are going to pass out, cold so bad you cannot feel your fingers or toes, cold so bad lines and valves around you are freezing up and breaking like an end of the world situation, then this book is dedicated to you.

I hope you enjoy this book and relate to it in many ways.

Chapter 1
How We Came to work in the Mills and Factories

I was raised in a small town in Northwest Indiana called Griffith. It was a rural community with mainly blue-collar families. My parents went through W.W. II and after the war settled down to raise a family. My dad was a chemical worker who worked in a chemical plant near by in the maintenance field. His true passion was racing motorcycles and midgets. I can remember going to the tracks as a child and watch him race, it was very exciting as a youngster! Eventually he had to give up racing. When I was fourteen he built me a go-cart and I had a lot of fun with it. This small town back then going to school was like typical life in America back then. In grade school I did the typical things kids did back then. In high school I took four years of high school college prep and four years of machine shop to get a well-rounded education. We did all the goofy things back then so many red blooded Americans did. We had camping poker parties near one buddy's house. I worked with my cousin in a janitorial business and one of the places I cleaned up was a bar so every week I would take beer and hide it all over Griffith in the tall grass by sign posts and when we would have a party I would drive all over and pick up the beer and we would have one heck of a poker party! I bought my dads old fifty-five Crown Victoria and he taught me how to restore and work on cars. Back then I had a neat looking hot rod and did a lot of things. I worked several jobs and always had enough money to do things, I did not know it but I was living the American dream. In high school our group was a mixture of greasers, brainiacs, and people of all types. We hung with the greasers for protection, the jocks for the girls, and the nerds for information. I told my buddies; that these are the best days because after high school you joined the military, went on to college, or got a job in the steel mills. Ironically that is how it did turn out.   A f t e r high school I went to Purdue Calumet, other friends went to college. To my surprise I flunked out the first semester. I took computer programming and had no clue to what I was doing. So I flunked out and went on to a junior college where I did much better. Being in the Viet Nam era I was drafted several times and managed to get a college deferment. Then I decided to join the Air Force and hopefully get a trade in the service. At the end of basic I aggravated an umbilical hernia I had and had the option of getting an operation. After much research with T.I.'s and seasoned people they told me to get out get a job and have it taken care of by an outside doctor. What convinced me was seeing a veteran sitting in a wheel chair with half of his head missing. The care of veterans back then was bad as it is today. They said they could only give me a 50/50 chance of curing it. After much research I opted to get out on an honorable discharge. After getting out I found out that the medical discharge kept me from getting a good job. I worked at a local golf course for several years. It was just like the movie Caddy Shack; Floyd the mechanic was Bill Murray. We did not make much money but we found golf balls to clean up and sell and had a good time working there. I later went to Indiana University to major in education where I flunked out of there. Determined, I went to Thornton Junior College then back to I.U. where a counselor told me to go to the steel mills, get an apprenticeship then go back to college later. I was at the point of no return, all these attempts of going to college and flunking out, working low paying jobs with no benefits and just existing. I talked to my wife and she talked to her father who was a supervisor in metallurgy and he told me to see a guy in the employment office. The day I went there I had an old Plymouth that overheated on the way there and made me a little late. By the time I got there I was a nervous wreck. I filled out application forms and took a mechanical test. Three days later I got a call to come in for an interview. He told me they had an apprenticeship program to become a mill mechanic in three and a half years with a job class rate of 18, the highest they had for a mechanic. In the older departments it would take 10 to 15 years or more to move up to job class 18. You would hire in and would work as a helper, building spares, cleaning parts, or carrying the tools for the senior millwright. You would be paid a low job class, maybe class 6 for 10 or 15 years until someone above you either died or retired. The mill mechanic trade was a combination of 11 trades into one, layout and burning, rigging, pumps and compressors, mill machinery, drafting, blueprint reading, etc. I gladly accepted the job and was sent to the head of maintenance for a final interview in one of Inlands top departments, the 80-inch hot strip mill. He asked me, with the college I had at the time, that after the apprenticeship I would stay with the company and I told him that I would stay. At that point I was hired.

The next Monday I reported to the main office at the hot strip mill at 6:30 in the morning and was given a tour, lists of clothes, boots, helmet, and all the equipment I would need. At this point I was just so exited to get into the mills and try to earn some decent money because I was basically poverty status. The steel mills and other manufacturing companies at that time preferred to hire relatives and friends of people already working at these companies. It was like a big family and everyone worked together. At that time in history, every shift change, it was like working in a big city with thousands of people coming and going. It was a far cry from what is left today of only a few hundred coming and going. There are four major steel mills in Northwest Indiana, one mill alone in 1979 employed 26,500 people. Today one mill employs maybe 6,000 people. The turnover in the mills back then was so great, that the week I hired in, the plant hired 500 people in one week with 75% of the hires to quit.

So I started working in the mill day shift until I was familiar with the department then they put me on shift work as they did all new hires. We were called "trainees" with an "x" on our helmet to let others know we just hired in. We wore these "x's for a month then they took them off. All the new hires hung around together as much as we could because the noise and environment was terrifying. When we could we would talk to each other about what we did and our lives and expectations in the mill. Talking to everyone we pretty much agreed that we were going to work in the mill long enough to earn money to go back to college, pay off bills, or to save money for something else. Once we got enough money then we were going to quit. Ah! The innocence of youth! Little did we know that most of us would stay there 30 years or more!

So after a 3-½ year apprenticeship, shift work, 6 days a

week or more, plus everything at home we all somehow got used to the fact that we were stuck in the mill. The first few years many of us were depressed that all our high hopes were dashed and the reality of the mill was terrible but it was a sense of a new life. We could earn a good living, get paid to go to college, and could even be trained in all of the industrial trades at company expense. It seemed overwhelming at first but it turned out to be one of the most fulfilling and best paying jobs we would have in our life times!

When I hired into the mill manufacturing jobs in this country were almost one fourth of the work force in this country. Anyone with a high school diploma could get a job and live the American dream. Today the only jobs there are in this country are fast food or department store jobs, paying minimum wage and no union or benefits. Steel mill jobs are less than one per cent of the work force in this country. Has our country become like the late Roman Empire who became so spoiled and lazy that they became complacent and had everyone else make everything for them? Has corporate America and the politicians gone too far with most of our manufactured goods made in foreign countries with cheap labor and huge profits only for the rich? Only time will tell.

Chapter 2
Basic Steelmaking from an Integrated Mill

This chapter deals with how steel is made. The mills I worked in are centered on the southern part of Lake Michigan. There are only a few other integrated mills left in this country. Some are out East with maybe one in southern Indiana and one in the Northwest of the United States. By integrated mills I mean a process that takes raw materials and makes either structural steel or sheet steel out of them. Structural steels are I-beams-angle-iron; square channel stock, rod-coiled steel, or steel with a special shape to it. The sheet steel is a flat-coiled roll that is unrolled at a plant to make appliances, automobiles, or other manufactured goods that require a flat surface that is usually formed in a particular flat or particular shape.

Years ago the older mills had coke plants that took coal, baked it in huge ovens and made coke out of it. This coke was combined with lime, iron ore, lime, and other ingredients and heated up in an open hearth. This open hearth poured the steel into large square blocks of steel that were later reheated and flattened into slabs called a bloomer. It was called this because these square shapes were called blooms. After the slab was made it was shipped on a train car to a hot strip where it was reheated and pressed down into a flat sheet coil. This coil then went to a cold mill for further processing or directly to the customer.

The newer mills today have a similar process but it is still a very complicated process.

First the coke used comes from a more modern day coke plant that pollutes less. When I first came to the B.O.F. the old coke plant was running next to us. You could smell the fumes coming from it a half mile away! At nighttime you could see the flames coming from the burning coke ovens and it looked like a scene from a Terminator sci-fi movie. There were stories of how people would put in for transfers to go to other cleaner departments and how their supervisors would block their transfers and keep them there. It was like being trapped in hell! After this coke plant shut down we worked with some of the people that worked there and all the horror stories were true. They had a fire there and when a gas valve blew up it killed two workers. The flames were so hot that you could feel them 200 feet away! There was a huge tank suspended in water that was going up and down fast. A coke plant employee told us that if that tank explodes it would destroy the bof, caster, and half of the blooming mill next to it. Fortunately the fire department showed up in time and finally got the fire out. The next week the supervisor that knew the valve was bad hanged himself at that valve because he felt that two of his coworker's deaths were his fault. Then I had a company camera to take pictures of ladle failures so I took several photos of the fire.

Miraculously some how a set of these pictures ended up in the union hall to help the fallen victims families get a just compensation.

Ore tankers brought in the other elements. These were ships as big as the oil tankers you see on television hauling oil all over the world. In the 70's the Edmund Fitzgerald was broke in half and sunk in a bad storm on Lake Superior. They hauled in iron ore from upper Michigan, Canada, and elsewhere. These elements were unloaded with huge self-unloading conveyors in the ships and piled on high mounds were they were transferred to the blast furnaces by long conveyors and trucks.

The blast furnaces were from 250 to 300 feet tall sticking up in the air spewing black clouds of steam and smoke. We had to go there for different parts and knew people working there. It was covered in a black suet that resembled an old coal-mining town, filthy beyond belief! These furnaces took these elements, coke, lime, ore, and other ingredients through a system of conveyors to the top of the furnace, and dumped them in. This was a hot liquid mass of molten metal suspended in the furnace called the "burden". With heating from either natural gas or kerosene this mixture when complete was poured out the bottom into large torpedo shaped cars called "pugh-cars". On rare occasions the furnace would lose their "burden" and they had to cool the furnace down and go in with burning torches and cut out the stuck metal. This would also resemble a scene from a horror movie! These "pugh-cars" could hold steel for 24 hours only before the steel would solidify and they would either have to be dumped or taken a part and the steel burned out. The hot metal in these cars was taken to a bof.

The basic oxygen furnaces, commonly called, B.O.F.'s were another gigantic operation. These buildings were at least a quarter of a mile long and approximately 350 feet tall! Scrap metal was brought in by huge dump trucks and dumped into large bays with various types of scrap metal in different bays. Scrap cranes with magnets took this scrap metal and loaded the scrap in huge scrap cars the size of a house. This car took the scrap box where a huge crane unloaded the box set it on a huge charger car that tilted the box and dumped it into the furnace. Several times these boxes would fall off these cars and maintenance would have to rig these boxes either back on the cars or have the charge crane load the scrap box into the furnace until the scrap car could be repaired. With the scrap in the furnace the charge crane would go to hot metal and pick up a ladle of steel the "pugh-cars" dumped into a 300-ton ladle. This ladle would then be poured into the furnace. Have you ever seen on TV a crane dumping hot metal into a ladle, it sounds like pouring water into it! The furnace would then be tilted upright, a water cooled skirt shield would be lowered to seal the top of the furnace, and a 40 foot lance would be lowered into the furnace to inject oxygen into the steel to mix it. Have you ever put a straw in pop or juice to blow into the straw and make bubbles, well that is the same principle they use to mix the steel. Also other elements are added to the steel in the ladle depending on the type of steel on the order. When the steel is mixed it is poured down to another steel ladle and is transferred by car and crane to a ladle metallurgy station where the steel is fine-tuned to an order. From there it is taken to the caster, set on a huge ladle machine, rotated, and poured into a mold where the shape of a rectangular slab is formed. It is then sent through a vertical to horizontal casting machine. Huge gas torches cut the slab into lengths then by railcar are transferred to a hot-strip where it is reheated and through a system of rolling mills is squeezed down to a thin steel strip that is coiled into a flat coil and is either shipped to a cold mill or directly to the customer.

There are also many departments in the mill that support the steel making departments. One department is a series of mobile equipment shops that repair and maintain the trucks, coil-carrying vehicles, mobile cranes, fork-lifts, man-lifts, and other types of mobile equipment used in these departments. Another department builds spares used by the main departments such as: air and hydraulic cylinders, hoses, rolls, and anything a department needs fast to continue operations. Other departments turn huge work rolls for rolling mills. Others build spare segments for casters. In general these service departments build spares that the steel making departments can get quickly to continue their operations.

As you can read this whole process of making steel is a massive and very complicated process, then again, it is like making homemade soup form scratch.

Chapter 3
The 80 Inch Hot Strip Mill

This chapter deals with the first department I worked in, commonly called "the mighty 80", because it was originally designed to make one and a half million tons of coiled steel a year and hit a peak of four and a half million tons of coiled steel in one year, after many upgrades and modifications and its workers. This mill was the only hot strip mill left running at the old Inland works in East Chicago. With the closing of many mills under the Reagan era and massive job losses in the manufacturing industry my company like many others shut down many departments. Most of the buildings you see driving by the plants are empty inside, used either for storage or parking.

This chapter deals with the people, the events that happened, and on the lighter side the antics of its workers.

This first person, I am only going to use nicknames or first names but anyone reading this book will either recognize that person or someone like him that they can relate to. Bill worked the recoil line, it was a mill connected to the 80 that took coils and either re rolled them or cut them to a certain width for the customer. Bill was a short skinny man with a weathered face and a funny sense of humor. He would have me go for coffee on the mill side, we would have a breakdown, and then we would either drink our cold coffee or walk all the way over to the other side again. That is how I got used to drinking cold coffee! He was a very good teacher, he would explain things or just tell you; now watch what I am doing. Then he would have you do it to make sure you paid attention. He must have been a hot roder at one time in his life because several times he would come in back of my truck go around me and cut in very close to me barely missing me by inches. One time he and two other workers were at a cabin Magoo had in Wisconsin. We called him Magoo because of the cartoon character because he could hardly see close up even with glasses. Some one called the cabin and said that Magoo's dad was sick and that they had to get back to Northwest Indiana fast. That was all Bill needed, he told his buddies hang on and have the change ready for the toll booths. Magoo came over to my house a nervous wreck with a six-pack of beer and a half pint of whiskey babbling of how Bill only slowed down enough to throw the money in the coin bin then race off again like he was in a Grin Prix race! They made a 3 1/2 hour trip in only 1-½ hours. Magoo found out his dad was all right and we kidded him about the experience for years after that. I saw Bill at work and he just said that he was just a "wus". Bill had a turbulent past with a lot of bad things that happened to him. He told me that if he had not came to the mill that he would either be dead or in prison but never the less he was a fine person that straightened his life out and became a colorful fellow coworker.

I met Bobby when I got to the last step of my apprenticeship;

you had to work on the hot mill; that is where they made the coils. He had a few more years' senority than I had and taught me many tricks about doing jobs the easy way. He was a very good mechanic, as were many of these people I worked with. He was from West Virginia and came to the mills like many of us, for the money. He said that in West Virginia there were a lot of poor people and the only jobs there were was in the filthy coal mines. He told me to learn all you can in the mill but don't be too good on the mill because then the office will keep you there and run you to death! He was right because that was one of the reasons I transferred to the caster later on. He would always tell me to pace yourself and realize that you have to be here at least 30 years before you could retire so work steady and keep busy. He would always tell me that we will make it to retirement and just take it all in at a steady pace. I saw him at our annual retirement party last year; we shook hands and the first thing he said," see; I told you we would make it to retirement"! In 1980 he transferred to a new blast furnace job as many of us would do later on because a young person back then had to have 25 years of senority or more to get a summer vacation or a steady day job.

    The next person I worked with on the mill was Bobby's old partner, J.T. He was a tall slender Black man with a kind smile that was one of the top mechanics on the mill. When things got hairy with a breakdown J.T. would always smile, look at you and say,"ah come on now". That would kind of relax you and he would always tell you now stick with me and do exactly what I tell you to do. When we would have a breakdown the foreman would always get him first, tell him what happened, then he would know exactly what to do to get the mill going again. One time a chain broke on a funace door, he borrowed a flame retardent coat from a furnace tender, put it on, and with a piece of sheet metal in front of him to block the flames and heat, hooked the door on the overhead crane with a cable, burned the remaining chain, and had the crane take the door away so they would not have to shut the furnace down or stop production. Back then the employees received awards for above ordinary acts to avert production delays or acts of maintenance that were done in a very short time. J.T. was one of these individuals who, like a fireman, would jump in the burning building and save the day. He was one of the best mechanics I worked with and an inspiring person to be with, always on a positive attitude. I saw him at our annual picnic two years ago and we had a good time talking about the old days. Sorry to say that he is no longer with us and is missed by all.

The next coworker is Jonsey, he was a big man with a heart of gold. He worked in many areas of the 80 like many of us did. He would talk to many workers with problems with his Southern background and common sense style only he had. He loved to eat, like many of us did, and could crack an egg with one hand on our many meals we would cook in the mill. When things would get out of hand he would always be the one that became the arbitrator and settle many disputes. He was a veteran and belonged to the veterans chapter in my old home town and was part of the honor guard. I still see him at the picnic and we always have a good time.

Another worker was Indian Joe, he told every one he was Indian and worked on the coilers. He would walk down the personnel tunnel or be at the coilers and yell out duck there coming! I asked him what is coming and he told me a flock of birds! I looked around and did not see anything, then he would say they missed us! Everyone told me he was nuts and to not pay any attention to him. Working with Joe on the coilers I learned a lot. He would cook breakfast in the morning on days and he would make a breakfast that was a feast! In one month alone I gained five pounds! His brother was a truck driver and would deliver in plant parts to us. We asked him if Joe was Indian, he laughed and said that he is Polish and that crazy act was so no one would bother him! I later saw Joe and he admitted it and told me that if you want people to not bug you let them think your crazy! I saw him at the picnic a couple of years ago and we went through ducking as if birds were flying over us, then we and every one just laughed.

Jonsey's buddy Herman; was a fun loving worker that always had a good time in the mill no matter what happened. He was a camera person and to this day always is taking pictures. The company had a short retirement plan that he had to let them know in one day if he wanted it. No one thought he would take it but he took it and retired to every ones surprise. Since then he has taken college courses and is still leading a full happy life.

The next worker is "Hambone", they called him that because he would eat almost anything and help people finish their lunches if they had too much. He would come up to you and say, "well; what are we eating today", to give you a hint to give him something to eat. He was a honest man and hated the "clicks" in the mill that so many work places have. He had a lot of kids and was there long after I left.

Next was Charley, he was a short sender worker, who took care of the loading and unloading of trucks coming into and leaving the 80. He was a great crane machinist and very good at coding spares and handling the many spare parts that came in and left the 80. The amount that came in and went out was staggering to see because of the thousands of parts it took to run this half-mile long complex. He taught us all many areas of the spares turnover in the department. He also was a good friend and was also a fellow hot rodder having a 67 427 corvette and a 55 Packard Patrician convertible. He also did road racing and we all got along good with him. He even transferred to the b.o.f. but went back before his 30 days were up. He later retired from the 80, went to work for a fabrication company and the last I heard he died of a stroke. He will be missed.

Next is Stubby; that was Charles's buddy, who also worked the docks. When his time was up he went back to working at the coilers, that is where they coiled the sheet steel into coils. He bought and rebuilt Cushman motorcycles and had quite a collection of them. They called him Stubby because he was short and had very short fingers that looked like little stubs. He was always busy and is still at the 80.

Next was Jimy, he originally came from the old open hearth and was the 80's top spares guru. If any one needed a part found or located he was the one to see. He taught all of us about gear teeth, blueprints, part numbers, and many other areas of the spares it took to run the department. He had a photographic mind and would remember things no one else could. He was a very good mechanic and a brilliant man. He also loved his beer and had his own named bar seat at a local tavern he would stop at after work.   Josephine was one of the women that worked in the office. She took care of apprenticeship testing, scheduling, and many areas of the mill. She would always help you if you needed something and was very kind and helpful. She was kind of our second mother at the mill because, for most of us that was our second home.
Hank was our expeditor for the main mill. He always some how got through all the turmoil and if they had a breakdown

STEELWORKERS: THE LAST OF THE BREED

he knew exactly what to do to get the mill going again. It was kind of funny talking to him because he would tell me when things got really hairy he would always have to take a trip to the machine shop way over in Plant 1 to just get away for a while. Jim was the expeditor for the auxiliary section of the department; that was all things that were not related to the main mill. He would always keep a cool head and tell me that I have the best job out in the mill because I was not stuck in the office turmoil that was an everyday occurrence at the 80. Several years later at the b.o.f. we had to go to a department that was almost closed down and we met again and reminisced of the old days. I told him that he made a good move getting out of the hectic 80. Bob worked the hot mill with many of us. He was always playing tricks on me and harassing me. He used to grab my shoulder blade, get his fingers under my shoulder bone and bring me to my knees. One day , after he found out that I was transferring out, I asked him who he was going to pick on and we looked up at a guy they called J.J. and I told Bob that he could be my replacement and he laughed and said, good choice. He would always help you if you needed help. We got to the point we would all tease some else on different days and it was just a camaraderie all of us had. It is like that in almost every workplace, everyone harassed each other but when any one needed help we would help each out. B i l l worked in the oil basement; that was where they had huge oil tanks that supplied all the oil used to lubricate the huge rolls that make the steel. It also supplied the massive water pressure on the nozzles to blow off the scale, a by product of heating the steel, in the many mill housings. He was a common sense type of guy who had a fascinating past. He was divorced, lived with one of his kids and and enjoyed being single. He had a Kowasaki motorcycle that was very fast. One night after

3/11's I was in back of him on the highway, he floored the gas and in a few seconds was just a little light spot on the highway. He told me he was doing about 120 mph! He was older than me by about 20 years and riding a motorcycle like that was amazing. I saw him at the picnic and he told me he was in the merchant marines in W.W.II and after retirement at the age of 65 he got several jobs on tramp steamers in the boiler room and traveled from Florida to Asia, South America, and all over the tropics. Quite a feat for a man of his age from Rolla Missouri where he retired!

Next is George, an immigrant from Serbia, like many people that came from foreign countries to America in search of a better life. He was the top mechanic technician on the main hot mill and built up the gear type spindles that connected the huge reductions to the work rolls that pressed down the steel in the mill stands. No one liked to work with him because he would yell at them if they did not do what he told them to do. So several times I got to work with him. You just had to do what he said and he had every tool you needed to work with. Workers would ask me how can you work with him and I just laughed and said at least he had all the tools you needed to do the jobs, because most of us had to go all over and borrow tools to do the jobs we had to do and a lot of times it took a long time. I used to kid him, he would teach me all the cuss words in Serbian, and the old joke is you learned all the cuss words in a foreign language then you were ready to learn the language. One day an outside company rebuilt two edger housings and delivered them to the mill. I looked at them and noticed they were built backwards and would result in a lot of trouble for the mill. George came up on his scooter and I told him, something is not right with those housings. He looked at them, opened his mouth, almost loosing his false teeth and ran right to the office and saved the day. I let him take the credit and the glory.

Next is George, who worked the oil basement with Bill and two other men. He was the technician there, each turn (shift) had one. When I first got there he taught me everything in the area. Later I found out that after he taught me then I was left to do all the work. That job was supposed to be an easy job and took a lot of senority to get. So after a year of so many complaints of my lack of sonority; that the office put me back on the mill. Actually they did me a favor because one of the older mechanics that complained of me got my job and later he told me that he runs you to death on that job. I just told him be careful what you wish for because you might get it! Have you ever had this worker envious of your job, complains to his boss, then gets your job only to find out it was not what he thought it was!

Next is our general foreman Harold, he was the head of the mechanical department. He was the last supervisor that worked his way up form the ranks to his position. He knew every part in the place and how to fix it. No one out there could pull the wool over his eyes because he knew better. One time he stayed out in the mill for 24 hours straight scraping babbit bearings; that was an old bearing material that was made out of lead and metal. It was used in the old days before roller bearings replaced them. He was the last person out in the mill that knew how to do it! We worked with him doing exactly what he said. At the end of a double shift we all went home. The next day when we came in we went to help him finish up and he was still there! That kind of dedication is rare today. After he retired the future department heads all had engineering degrees. He was the last of a dedicated breed who; did what ever it took to keep the department going and never complained!

The last supervisor was Jerry, a short little Polish immigrant that spoke with broken English. It was hard to understand him some times, so you would have to ask him just to show you what he wanted you to do. Sometimes we would make fun of his accent and duplicate his broken language. If he caught you he would constantly be riding you for six months! One time he had his head in between two spindles and the operator brought them down on his head. He had blood coming out of his ears and they asked him if he wanted to go to the hospital and he told them, what for. The next day he came out as if nothing ever happened! He was a little man with the constitution of a giant.

These are just a few of the people that worked there so hopefully reading about them would give you an idea of perhaps someone you are or have worked with at one time or another.

This next part of the 80, deals with the roof cave in. There is a roll shop, called no. 5 roll shop that resurfaces the work rolls and back-up rolls for the main hot mill stands that presses down the slabs into sheet steel. It is a huge area and is a separate department with in the main hot mill. There are several roll shops located through out the vast complex of different departments. They are under the control of a central roll shop department and they do all their maintenance and work in the roll shop department.

One winter it was very cold and we had a lot of snow, I think it was around 1977.

At that time period the mills had their own building inspectors who inspected the buildings. They would inspect the sheet metal siding, roofs, water lines, and all areas connected to the operation of the various departments. Since the steel mills started downsizing in the 80's I do not know if they have these people today.

It was on the start of a midnight turn. I had just got to the shop and went to the roll shop to get a cup of coffee. I sat down in the auxiliary shanty peeling an orange and drinking my coffee when I looked out the door window and saw what looked like an avalanche coming down on the roll shop I was just in! The crane hot rails exploded in a loud thunder and for about fifteen minutes you could not see any thing but a huge cloud of gray dust coming from the roll shop. I jumped up ran outside the shop and could not believe my eyes! The roll shop I was just in was covered in ice! The roll racks, roll build-up area, and the entire south part of the roll shop was buried! I ran into the office to tell my supervisor but no one was there. I ran into the coiler pulpit to tell the supervisor there and he called down to the finishing mill pulpit to tell them what happened. A couple of my coworkers heard the crash and we grabbed fire extinguishers and ran to the roll shop. All we could see was a huge 200 foot wide or larger hole where the roof was. The roof, trusses, lighting, all were gone! Then they shut down the mill and people were all over the place looking to see if anyone survived! The main mill supervisor had us look for broken bolts on the walkway that feel down on the personnel walkway. He informed all overhead cranes to stay away from the adjoining building because the broken bolts could be from the columns and they were afraid the cranes could come crashing down. We looked as best we could but the ice over the roll shop was at least 30 feet deep! We could not find any survivors and we feared the worst. All of the department heads, managers, and supervisors were immediately called from home and came out. The area that I had just got a cup of coffee was covered completely in 30 feet of ice! Had I been there five minutes later I would be dead! They found out after a couple of hours that it was shift change and the roll shop was empty! Had it been just a couple of minutes later and several people would have been killed! It was a miracle! They had helicopters fly over the shop the next day and estimated that 150 tons of ice formed on the steam vents for the hot mill. When that ice broke loose it was like an avalanche crashing through the roof taking everything with it in its path! The next day an outside company and a couple supervisors had to go on the roof with dynamite and blast the rest of the ice away! Then the huge job of cleanup started. With tractors, cranes, and outside ironworkers they had to clear out the ice first then begin taking and hauling away the damaged equipment. Then outside ironworkers began installing new roof trusses, sheeting, electrical lines, and all of the things that were in the building before it was destroyed. It took many months to rebuild and get everything working again. In the mean time the other roll shops had to do the work the No.5 shop did. The two roll shop cranes were spared because they parked them at opposite ends of the building. At that time period they had huge heaters in the buildings for heat. With a gaping 200 foot hole in the roof the winter winds blowing off Lake Michigan soon froze everything up! The whole area was as cold as it was outside! An older mechanic told me this was nothing; wait till it warms up. A couple weeks later it warmed up and all the steam and water lines had frozen and split. When these lines thawed they started gushing water and steam all over the place! At one point there was at least three inches of ice on the floor and you had to really watch your step. Then the two entrance doors to the shop broke and it was like a wind tunnel with the winds coming down the roll shop and going out the two broken doors! I got sick the last couple of days working in all that cold. I had a vacation coming then and we went out West to California. With all that happening I was tempted to look for a job there and move there but I did not for some reason. As it turned out I was the only one to actually see the roof cave in and to this day it was one of the worst disasters at the company I worked for!

The next incident was when Frank, Johnny, and myself; were removing the pusher pins so we could get an overhead crane and remove a giant furnace pusher to rebuild it. Any damaged steel was replaced, cracks were cut out and welded, and new wear liners were installed. These furnace pushers were about three feet high and were about 30 feet long. Huge pins would hold these pushers in place and were about three feet long and about one foot six inches thick and very heavy. A stack of slabs, about six or seven high, were lowered onto a depillar that lowered and pushed off one slab at a time, ran them down a roll line, then with these pushers, usually two at once, pushed the slabs into the furnace. As these slabs lined up into the furnace they were heated red hot, usually to about 1700 degrees Fahrenheit. Then as the slabs were needed were pushed out one at a time to be processed in the mills.

We took off the keeper bolts on the pins and installed an eyebolt on the end of the pin. Then a cable was attached to the eyebolt, through a com a along or also called a chain-jack, then that device was attached through another cable to a pusher to pull out the pin. A third cable was attached to an overhead crane to hold the pin as it was pulled out. We hooked everything up and proceeded to pull out the pin. As the pin was pulled out half way we put a cable around the pin to hold it with the crane. At that moment the pin all of a sudden popped out, slid off the cable the crane was holding it with, came off the come a long slammed down on a drive coupling. Frank just stood there stunned and starred at the pin. Johnny was in back of the pin out of the way. I was directing the crane and in the direct path of the pins travel. For a fraction of a second they say you can see your life passing before you. I could see a vision of crushed thighs on my legs. I turned and started running down the steps toward a hand railing. When I got to about a foot and a half from the railing I stumbled and feel down. The pin rested on that coupling for about two seconds, rolled down the steps, crushing every metal end insert on the ends of the steps then came to rest about a foot and a half away from me! Had I not feel I would have jumped over the handrail and feel about fifteen feet and probably would have been hurt. Had the pin stayed on the come a long it would have pinned Frank across his body at an angle and hurt him badly. We all took a break and talked about it; then proceeded to take the other pin and pusher out. This situation scared us badly but we regrouped and proceeded on as mill workers always do. It was a miracle no one was killed or hurt! This was just another incidence that this job was a very dangerous occupation, but some one had to do it.

The next part is the power outage that happened one night at the 80 inch hot strip mill. It was on a 3/11 turn, or commonly called an afternoon turn or shift. We were doing our normal work on the hot mill when all of a sudden we heard an explosion that sounded like it came from the West where the slab yard and power station is located. All of a sudden the lights went out and everything stopped. There was quiet in a normally extremely loud environment! You could hear everyone running around and yelling to one another. The emergency lighting turned on but they were very dim compared to what we were used to. We turned our flashlights on and went up to the finishing mill pulpit to report to the senior mill foreman Kenny to see what happened and he did not know himself. He told us to go to our trailers and wait for further instructions. As we walked to our home bases you could look down the mill line and see a red glowing slab that was just getting ready to go into R-5, the last of the roughing mills. It's glow looked like an eerie sci-fi movie of an apocalyptic disaster glowing in the back of the tall mill housing. We all looked at it and agreed that we were lucky that not one slab was stuck in any of the mill housing when the power went out. Otherwise we would have to burn them out with huge torches, plus all of the grease and oil on these mills for certain would have caught fire creating a very dangerous situation for all of us. We finally found out that a transformer blew up in the slab yard. The company found one in Texas but it would take at least four days to ship it here! They calculated the mill would be down for at least a week. They sent the production people home and set up fire watch maintenance crews to watch the place in this dimly lit, only by emergency lights and a few power generators that were brought in to give some light in the different areas of the mill. So we would come out on our regular shifts and patrol our assigned areas to make sure there was no; flooding, fires, or anything that would cause harm to any personnel or equipment. That is when to this day at home I still have flashlights in my vehicles, the house, and the garage. You had to use your flashlight to patrol these areas so it was critical to have good batteries and a good flashlight! If you could hear the eerie quite, water dripping, and the pitch dark in a once thriving well lit department it was very strange, like being in a cave at the deepest part of it with the eerie silence that goes with it! After one week the department's electric was restored and it began producing steel again. It was strange to see it alive again with all of the deafening loud sounds a hot strip mill makes in making steel. It was an experience that all of us would never forget.

On the lighter side steel workers in that time era did many things. There were pot smokers who would roll their joints up on the school desks before a break in apprenticeship school. There was even a rumor that they built a long swing over the tall roof between the slab yard and the motor room roofs. They would go up there smoke their pot and get in that swing and swing over the roofs about 40 feet in the air! It was common to smell pot on the runway of a crane during a wheel change! I never did because I told them that if you make one mistake 40 feet up it could get your coworker or yourself killed or hurt. One night on a 3/11 shift they brought in some brownies that had pot in them and gave some to older workers. One just sat in the bearing shop the whole shift and just stared at the walls! Then there were the ones that drank alcohol but most of them waited until they got to there vehicles or the bars to unwind. It was a harsh environment and for many it took all they had to get through their shifts safely then unwind when they left. That era was in the 70's and 80's and much of that is gone today in the mills. With these good paying jobs dwindling and drug screening of new employees companies today want the best workers they can get and much of that on the job antics are gone today in a much more serious business environment.

Steelworkers, like many hard physical jobs, love to eat. Mainly on 3/11 shifts and the weekends we would pick a day, decide what we were going to eat and everyone would bring in a food item or donate the money and someone would buy all the food and bring it in. One 3/11 shift we all decided to have a taco feast. We all brought in food items and our ex griever did all the cooking while we did all our job assignments and took care of the mill calls. When we all came into the shanty to eat we were treated to a feast you could not get at a good taco restaurant! The whole table was full of food! We had everything from pork tacos, goat cheese, lettuce, tomato, tortillas, refried beans, jalapenos, taco chips, and more! We all ate our share and still had leftovers! I alone ate 17 tacos! Our welder ate and just said he could not believe it. Today he has been the president of our union for many years and has done a fine job for all of us. Then we had a call to take a furnace rood off. We went to the furnace and took the two roofs off but we could hardly bend over but we did our job. There were other areas that had their designated cook. One person on the coilers always had a pot of chili or stew cooking and anyone was welcome to help them selves. We took care of our selves like people in the military or other jobs that were unique to where only these people shared in job that was different from normal. We would also donate money, clothing, and other items needed by society. For instance one fall we donated and brought to a where house winter coats for the Lakota Indians in South Dakota to help them brave the severe winters out there. .

One winter, I think it was 1982, we were working 3/11 shift and the weather forecast was for severe cold temperatures. The different mill stands had steam spewing from them as they pressed down the red hot slabs like a huge steam geyser coming out of the ground like Yellowstone's "Old Faith full"! Water valves on the mill and slab yard side were bursting and spewing water all over the place! They had to keep the mill rolling at all cost because if it broke down everything would freeze up and that would take a long time to repair. Out side you could see the steam billowing from the steam lines and the vents on top of the buildings. The mill was right on the lake and in the winter time when the temperatures dropped it was like living in Antarctica! Near the end of the shift the mill foreman asked some of us to double over to midnights to repair broken lines. Setting at the table in the shanty was a newspaper predicting the temperatures to drop to 23 below zero with estimated wind chills of 85 below! Most of us knew this would be a nightmare and turned him down, but a few that desperately needed the money accepted. That night I agreed to give a co-worker a ride home. We all showered walked outside to the gatehouse. Buy the time I got to the gatehouse my mustache was frozen solid and we all had to stay there for a while and warm up! We got to my truck and I started it up and for three minutes it just rattled and shook! The only light that worked on the dash was the break light! Then the oil started to circulate and the gauges and everything started to work! I took him home and that night and his mother was so happy that I brought him home she gave me a plate of home made tacos to take home. That night it was one of the coldest nights on record with wind chills of 85 degrees below zero! Four of the storm windows in my house cracked but luckily we all got through it!

    Another winter, I think it was close to this time; in the early eighty's I was working auxiliary. That area is not the main mill but includes all the cranes and equipment that is not directly related to the main mill. We were on calls and got a call from a crane man saying his trolley was getting stuck and could not move. We knew right away that it was ice on the trolley rails. His crane, as luck would have it, was an outside gantry crane that picked up the slabs off of the train cars and piled them up in stacks of ten or more high. Then again it was winter with howling winds coming out of the north off of Lake Michigan with a bone chilling wind chill! We had to climb a series of ladders inside the structure of the crane to get to the top of the crane where the trolley was. We got to the top of the crane, pulled the main hot rail switch, and locked it out. We then proceeded to climb around the hot rails and started chipping off the ice on the rails with a welders chipping hammer. We were about 80 feet above the ground and you had to brace your body to compensate for sudden wind gusts of over fifty miles an hour! If you would get blown off of the crane at that altitude it would mean certain death! We got the ice off and had the crane man run the trolley and it ran good so we climbed back down and went to the shop to warm up. Words cannot describe the bone chilling cold atop that crane! We just joked and said, " that is why we make the big bucks". If any of you ever did a job something like this it would make you envy an office worker that just had to worry about paper cuts!

In closing on the 80 inch I would also like to mention these men and women, yes there were a few women mill mechanics in other departments; that made things out of nothing! They would make hand rails out of pipe and angle iron. They would make door hinges and handles out of pipe couplings and bolts. They would repair damaged conveyors with a torch, metal, and a good welder. They would get out broken bolts by welding a flat washer to the bolt, then weld a nut to the flat washer, then using a wrench or impact take out the broken bolt. I always kidded every one that we could go to Iraq or Afghanistan and make things work out of anything because that is what we did in the mill all the time. Also we learned in apprenticeship school to calculate the size of an impact socket needed by taking the bolt diameter, add one half the diameter, for the bolt head, then at one eighth for the nut size. Many of these things we learned might be lost forever in this so called high-tech world we live in today and we might become a mystery like how they built the pyramids years ago!

Chapter 4
2B.O.F. 2Caster

This chapter deals with one of the last new departments the former Inland Steel Company built at the Indiana Harbor works in East Chicago, Indiana. With the desire for the American steel industry to go to all cast steel like the Japanese and the Germans, the company bought and built 2 Caster. It was 100 per cent cast steel; this process eliminates an open hearth and all the many processes that go with ingot steel. Cast steel is exposed less to air and impurities and produces a better grade of steel. With all of the American steel equipment makers going bankrupt in the 80's the only countries left to buy steel mill casters and equipment from were the Japanese, Germans, and the Swedish.

With nothing to look forward to but shift work, winter vacations, split days off, and always being at the bottom sonority wise many of us put in for a transfer. Much to our amazement many of us were accepted, interviewed, and started working in the caster in the summer of 1985. This was six months before it started up. It was amazing seeing a new clean department with an army of workers from all over working there. We attended caster schools of all the components that went into the operation and maintenance of the new caster. For once we were taught preventative maintenance from the start up of the department and the proper procedures of maintenance. The older departments practiced preventative maintenance but somehow it was down played as the departments got older and had more break downs. This department was to be the show case for the rest of the company to follow. If this department was successful the rest of the departments would follow to get their preventative maintenance programs back to a higher standard.

So we attended many classes for several months on the operation of the caster, what did what, where everything was located, the procedures of taking equipment apart and assembling it back to specifications, and the complete process of taking a hot ladle of steel and pouring it into a caster to get a slab at the end of it. There were also free lunches and several company dinners from outside vendors trying to get supplier contracts from the new department. To us it was great although many of us put on several pounds with all of the free food!

We also worked with the outside iron workers and construction crews on several projects on the caster. One day Jose and I were working on a coupling alignment of a wire feeder assembly and we heard a huge scuffle coming from the ladle track rails. It was about fifty construction workers fighting and yelling and throwing things all over! Then we saw about five plant guard cars pull up at once with all of the guards getting out and stopping the fight. Later we found out that some of the workers were doing the union jobs someone else should have been doing. They were all told they were fired for that day and went to the bars to vent their anger. The next day they showed up and worked together all day as if nothing happened!

We also worked with workers from Japan, Germany, and Sweden. We mainly worked with the Japanese and Hiromira, a representative from Nippon Kokan Steel Company in Japan, because they were the main supplier of caster equipment left in the world and had the latest technology. Hiromira told us that the Japanese are taught in their steel mills that everyone does a specific job and does it well. We told him here in America that we are taught many jobs and do above and beyond what we are taught in the steel mills and everyday life. He said people in Japan only make about 20'000 thousand dollars a year. They have apartments instead of houses, their utility bills are only about 25 dollars a month, they spend their money on clothes and dining out, and they buy a new car every five years because it is a disgrace to have an old rusty car in Japan! The people from Sweden and Germany told us about the same story. Then we puffed out our chests and told them that we make about 40;000 thousand dollars a year, twice what they make. Then we kept talking and found out that after we paid our: house payments, utilities, grocery bills, car payments, doctor bills, college, income tax, sales tax, state tax, etc. we made less clear money and saved less money than they did! This was a lesson they taught us in humility. The once great American steel industry now had to rely on foreign countries to buy their steel mills from! After we realized this then we got along fine. We had a pizza party and Hiromira could not believe how much pizza we could eat! We told him in Japan you have a casting machine and in America we have eating machines! We all laughed. He told us that when they were done here they were going to China and to build five casting machines with more to come later! He told us that a country and mankind must first learn how to crawl, then walk, then run and that China was just getting started like our country was in the 1930's! We had also worked with a man from Germany. Knowing some Spanish and bits and pieces of other languages one day I came up to him telling him good morning and how are you in German with an accent! This man looked at me amazed and started rattling off German like he was my brother! I told him in German that I only spoke just a little. Then his excitement went away and we all just laughed because he realized that it was only a harmless joke. We had many good experiences working with these people from all over the world and it made us realize that we were no different from any other country, just working people trying to earn a living for our families and live a good life.

This segment deals with the people of 2 B.O.F. 2 Caster. With all of the departments closing down and many workers looking for a better department to work in many of us put in for transfers to the new caster.

Wally was from the 4 Slab mill. He, like many workers heard rumors of it closing down and looked for a better department to work in. He had a great sense of humor and like many of us had been through a lot. We appointed him tour guide and we would take tours of the new caster as it was being built to familiarize ourselves with the new equipment. We used to call these tours Wally World tours after the Chevy Chase movie " Wally World", because it reminded us of an amusement park with all of the equipment and the rides we would take on the new equipment. He used to kid us that after working here he would never go to "Disney World" again because he worked in one every day and was paid for it!

The next person was Herby, who lived in Black Oak, named

after the black oak trees that grew there. Herby, like many others, that lived there were from the South and moved up here for the jobs. He was a simple man with a lot of common sense and you got the idea that he did not know too much until someone did something to him or tried to trick him then he let you know he was much smarter than you thought! We had a lot of fun going to the new caster training schools with all of the free lunches and free items we received; it was truly the honey moon before the caster started up! He loved his beer and his buddies would all get together at the bars and have a good time. He started racing dirt track cars at a local clay track and got his kids interested in racing. Once his kids got the racing bug he quit racing and supported his kids. He admitted to us that he did this to give his kids something to do to keep them out of trouble and it worked!

The next person was Nash; he was from the 100 Inch Plate Mill. This mill was rumored to close down for years so he figured that it was time to go. When this mill shut down it was the only rope drive mill left in the United States and the main flywheel rope drive ended up in the Smithsonian Institution! I went to high school with him and when we all showed up at the caster we were amazed because we had not seen each other in 30 years! He and I worked together a lot in the caster because we worked slow and did a job right the first time. Other younger workers would rush the job to impress bosses and to get a better job. They would all make fun of us taking a long time doing a job then we would both laugh at them because they rushed through the job and left out something and had to go back and redo everything! We got a job building up spares and maintaining roll coolant rolls. At first no one wanted the job because it was in such bad shape. After a while making hand tools and rebuilding everything it got to be a good job.

Then fellow workers started complaining that they wanted the job. Then our boss gave them the job! We joked with everyone that we were the Special-High-Intensity-Training crew and no one wanted our jobs until all the bugs were worked out! Have you ever had a job like that where someone made fun of you then when you straightened the job out every one wanted it, well it happened to many of us in our working careers!

The next person was Kevin; he was from the 2 Bloomer Mill next to the caster. He also left it for the rumored shut down that happened shortly after the caster started up. He was a simple man and kind of quiet. This was only a disguise because if he could ketch you off guard and play a joke on you he would do it in a minute! He used to play jokes on one of the former machinists that transferred to the caster. We would kid him asking him what joke he played on the guy for that day. We tried to tell this machinist that if he could get you mad he was going to do it all the time. We told him just to shrug it off but he never could.

The next person is Rich, he was originally a machinist for an in the plant group of people that performed various mechanical and electrical duties for all of the departments at the Indiana Harbor Works. He worked on overhauling equipment and bringing them back to original specifications. When the mills began downsizing in the 80's many of these separate departments laid people off. These people went through apprenticeships to become a mill mechanic or to become another trade in the mills. It was a lot to go through but they had to relearn new trades to stay in the mill for the money and benefits. Rich was one of these people. He was a good bowler and always bowled on a league and always had a lot of jokes to tell. He would keep us briefed every week on the latest jokes, news, stock market, or other events. He was very smart and always kept up on current news. Any time you needed to know something specific on a machinist question you could ask Rich, if he did not know he could direct you to someone that did know. The mills, at that time, had most of the knowledge on the working floor of the departments. If you wanted to know anything you would ask Rich or someone and if they did not know they could direct you to someone who did know! It was an amazing source of knowledge!

The next person was Bill; he was hired and trained as a welder. These welders were the last of a dying breed also because all they did was weld. In the 90's the company began training mechanics as mechanic welders to both welding and mechanical work, like getting two trades for the price of one. Bill was a welder only and made this clear right off the bat. When the caster first started up every one had to rotate for six months on shift work to fill in the gap of maintenance on the night and week end shifts. They put Bill and I together to set us up because they knew Bill would not do any mechanical work and I would be the only mechanic in the caster on the off turns! We would get a call to come up to the casting floor by the casting foreman. He would be all excited and tell us he wanted this and that and I would calmly tell him that I was the only mechanic out in the whole caster. I would see the look on his face go from excitement to despair as he would say; well there are two of you. I would calmly tell him that Bill is a welder, not a mechanic, so if you have a small job I can do I will be happy to do it or otherwise it will have to wait till the day crew can do it. This turned out to work well for us and we made the best of a potentially bad situation. Bill also had fun on the shift work job. One July 4th he brought out several bottle rockets and shot them out of a pop bottle at all kinds of things in the caster. We had to work on the holiday so we made our own celebration. Bill would do things that no one expected as if to go against the rules, like many of us did in the 70's. He one night, he brought a barbeque unit into the lunch room and cooked us steaks over mesquite chips and all! He would even agree to work over time so his friend would not get it, stay two hours and go home, then the next day tell his fellow welder that he went home just to get him mad! Bill is still at the mill today and is keeping every one out there on their toes!

Another welder was called Dan, he, Bill, and Roy were the last of the welders that did welding only. Dan got to work in the morning and trained everyone to go by his schedule. If he had to go on a job right away he would, but if he did not have to he would delay as long as he could; doing a job. He was smart because he created a nuisance on purpose so you would go to another welder and leave him alone. Most of the time this worked but if he had to go he would. He was called, "the doctor of weld", because he would always do everything by the book and make sure everything was done the right way! He is still at the mill today keeping every one going!

The next person is Rich, he was a no nonsense person that just wanted to do the work and did not want the drama that the other jobs had like foreman, planner, or inspector. He was a vet that had been through a lot and had a very good sense of humor. We used to say that the world was full of crazy people and to only hang out with the few left that were not crazy. When we came to work in the crane area of the B.O.F. he was very helpful to us and showed us how to repair the many unique cranes they had there. I saw him at the picnic and he had just retired like many of the older workers around the country are doing and we just joked of the days when we had to go into the work world and endure all kinds of circumstances!

STEELWORKERS: THE LAST OF THE BREED

The next person is Rene; he transferred to the B.O.F. from the #2 Bloomer Mill next door because of rumors of it closing down, which it did. He was a Viet Nam vet that saw action and was wounded. He talked about it a little but did not make a big deal about it. He was a technician in the old department and transferred to the new complex like many of us did. He was one of the original group of inspectors that the company trained to be the technical experts in the mechanical field in the mill. The departments also had inspectors in every section of the maintenance field. The inspectors had many duties: coupling alignment, oil samples, vibration readings, equipment inspection, failure analysis, water samples, and many other areas of preventative maintenance. The goal was to insure that the equipment would be reliable during the process of making steel. Rene went to all of these schools and learned the areas well and trained us later inspectors in the various areas. He was a good teacher and had a lot of patience in teaching us the actual application of the things we learned in school to the job itself. He gave many of us insight on why equipment broke down and how to prevent it from breaking down the next time. He later retired and got a job in building maintenance near his home. I see him at the picnic and he is doing fine.

One of the more color full workers was Sam. He transferred from the open hearth to the B.O.F. right after it started up in 1974. He knew most of the equipment at the B.O.F. He was also in at least two severe accidents, one involving a train that hit his car, and a motor cycle accident. Both of the accidents almost killed him. Both of these accidents put him in a coma for weeks and it was a miracle he was still alive! He talked slow and did everything like in slow motion. Most of the people made fun of him. They would make fun of him until he got mad enough to fight then would beat him up. It is hard to believe grown men could do this but then again the harsh environment changed many people in the mill, some for the better; some for the worst. I met Sam when I was transferred from the caster to the B.O.F. and he would explain to me these different areas of the department. He was quiet and ate quite a lot of food for being as skinny as he was. He told me about the accidents and that they made fun of him because of the way he talked. I found out that he was quite knowledgeable in business, current events, math, and many other things. I think that is why they made fun of him because these other employees were jealous of him because he was a well versed in finance, economics, and many other areas that they were not. I told Sam that he had all of his investments in order and all of his bills paid that when he got 30 years in the mill to retire and go do what he liked doing. Seeing him at the picnic that is exactly what he did. We used to joke that the people that made fun of him are still at the mill and he is out on retirement! We got to be good friends and worked together many times and shared a lot of good times. I went to his house several times, met his wife and all of the pets they had. It just goes to show you that, "you cannot judge a book by its cover" and "never judge someone until you walk in their shoes". We still see each other at the annual picnic and he is doing fine.

The next person is Juan, a short stocky person that walked slow and did not talk much. Juan transferred from the other B.O.F. in the plant and worked in the caster until he also was transferred to the B.O.F. He also was assigned the crane area because the regular B.O.F. people did not want the area because all of the climbing involved and the harsh weather one had to put up with. We started working together and would argue because he would move slow and wait for me to do something. We would argue and I would get mad and he

The following ten photos are of the plant #2 Coke Plant fire where two steel-workers were killed (approximately 1998).

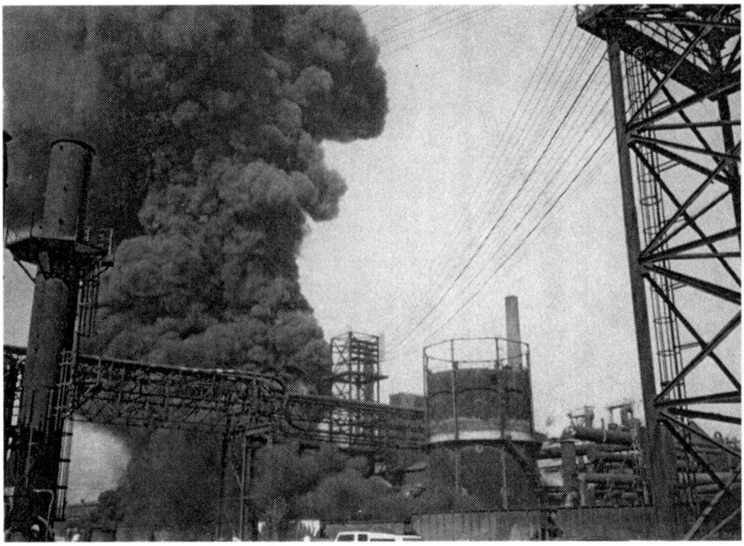

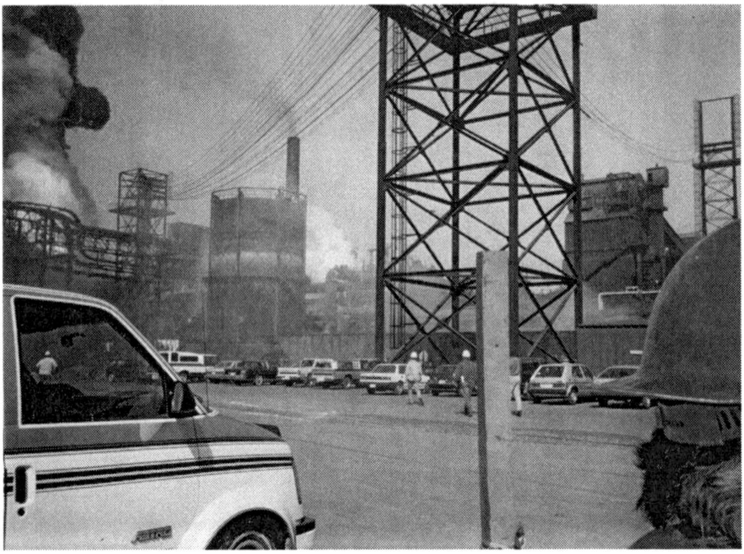

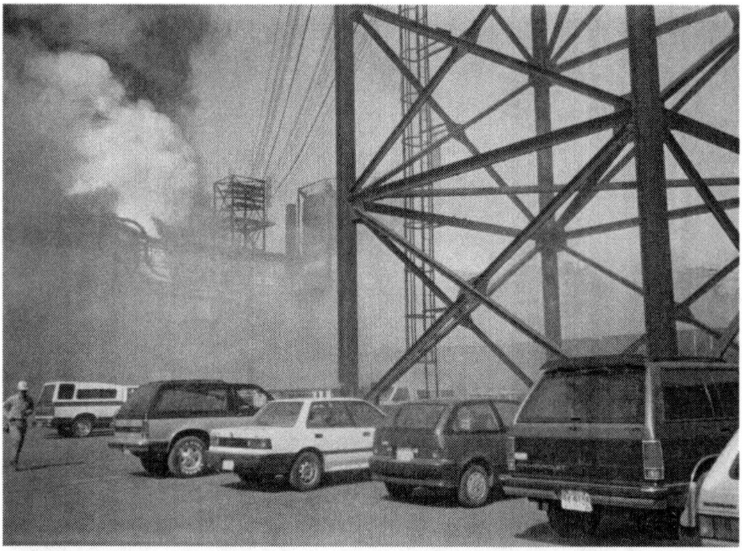

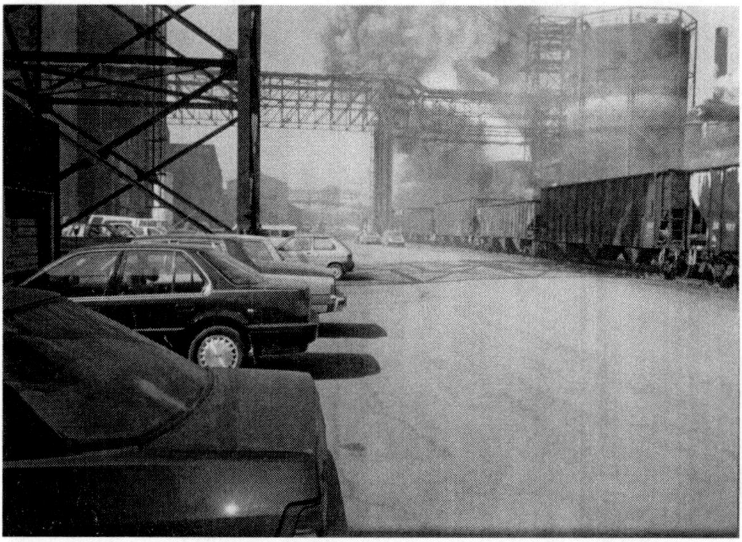

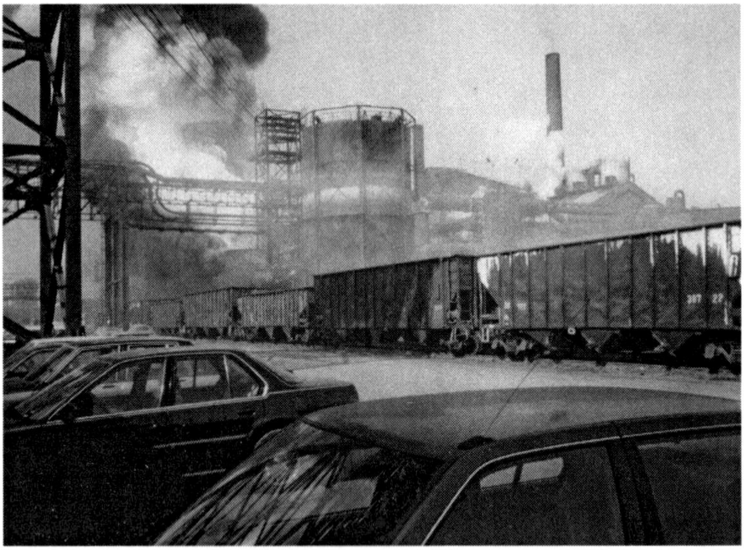

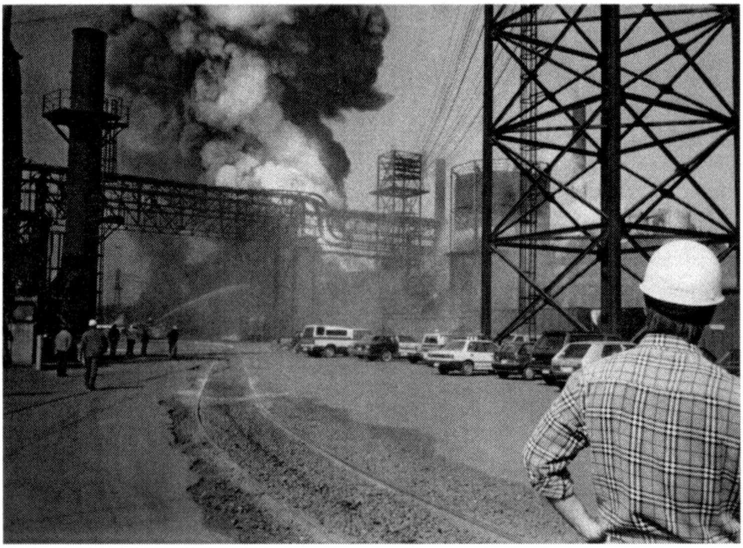

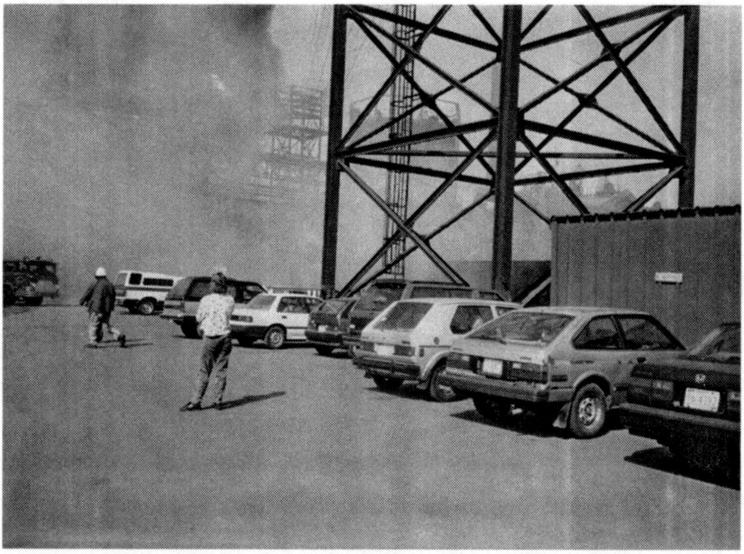

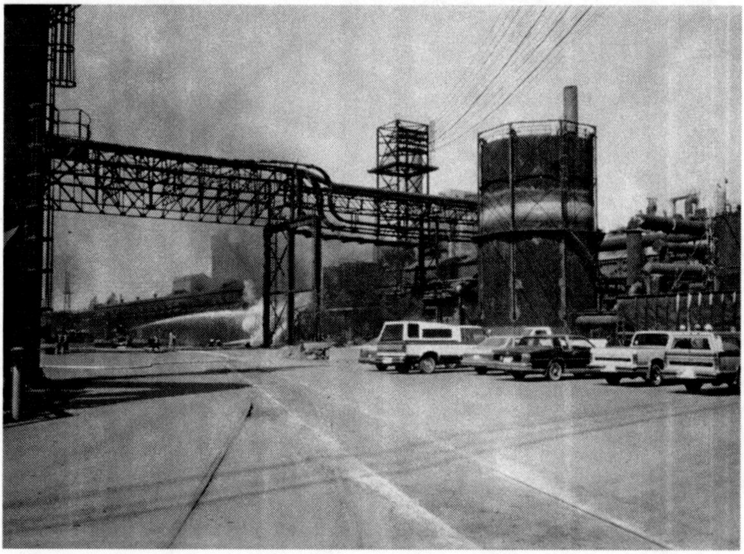

#2 caster lunchroom taken 1987 (see Chapter 4)

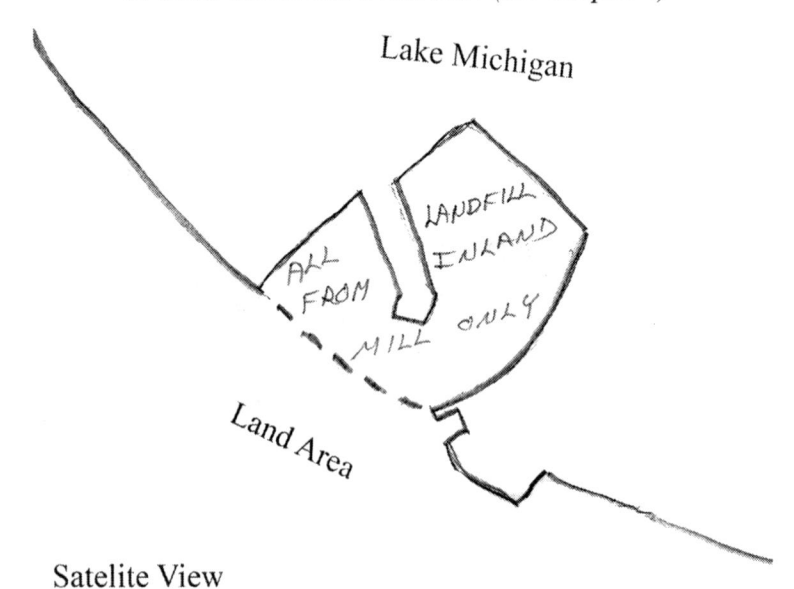

Lake Michigan

LANDFILL INLAND
ALL FROM MILL ONLY

Land Area

Satelite View
This picture is hand drawn by me to show the large amount of land fill these mills created. This is in land steel only.

Employee annual picnic, late august, 2009 Crown Point, Indiana

This picture is of a steel ladle and the brick being broken out by a "jitter-bug-tractor" so it can be relined with new brick

told me that I would have a stroke someday the way I got mad. Well six months later I ruptured a maxillary artery and came within one day of bleeding to death! After I came back to work they put us working together again as if to taunt us. We started talking and I found out that he was a foreman at the B.O.F. and that he would run all over the place in the faced paced environment that they had. He had a heart attack, they placed a pace maker in his chest, and later removed it when his heart beat was regulated. He told me he could see me getting ready to blow something and tried to warn me but I did not listen. After I got back to work I felt that I got a second chance. We just worked together at our pace and got to be good friends. At the time I was smoking a lot and he also did when he had his heart attack. Since then he quit and I have cut down to almost nothing. I had Spanish in high school and college and we spoke Spanish on the job so that the people that made fun of us could not understand us. It was our way of getting back at them without any violence. He told me about his brother that lived in Mexico in the mountains. He had six children and they were poor. He described that his children all had chores; no one argued over their duties, no one complained about having anything. They would all get together for meals, would be grateful for what they had, respected and looked up to their parents and all got along together. Juan told me about his children that they did not get along, one was jealous of the other, and in general they were not close as a family at all. I told him that sounds like the typical American family today. We joked about how the younger children did not appreciate what they have today.

Juan is still at the mill today and doing fine. Then again he is another person that is much different than what he looks like.

The next person is Pat, who was born in Alabama but grew up in Black Oak. He came from modest beginnings and got a job in the mill like most of us did. He learned how to work on cars in the 60's like a lot of us did. With the training in the mill as a mechanic and the love of hot rod cars he went into the business of fixing up and selling cars on the side out of the mill. He used to kid us he came from a poor section and was just trying to make it. He was one of the most knowledgeable people to go to for information on how to do any type of work on an automobile and was held in high regard in this field. He would take parts off of junk cars, do his magic, and assemble another car that was a complete beautiful hot rod then sell it at a profit. The only car he kept was a Thunderbird that he fixed up himself from the ground up. He came by my house one night in his 56 T-bird and we went to a car show. The car only had 50 miles on the new restoration and rode like new! The last I heard of Pat he retired from the mill and started rehabbing houses and was doing fine.

The next person is RD, also who came from Alabama up to Northwest Indiana for the manufacturing jobs that used to be abundant up there. He was very short, only about five feet tall. I like most people from European descent, was short. I was only five feet five inches tall and I used to kid him that us short people had to stick together! He was a veteran of Viet Nam and had combat experience and would only talk about it if he got to know you and no one else was around. He also got into buying and selling cars while working in the mill to get ready to do this when he retired. He also did some body building and kept in good shape. He also was a knowledgeable person to ask any questions about motorized vehicles. The mill was like that when we worked there. I used to kid people that all the knowledge is on the mill floor with the workers. You could go to the right person and find out anything from computers to body work! RD also retired and I saw him at a hot rod meet and he is doing fine.

These then are just a couple of the hourly workers in this department. I could go on farther but this will give you a cross section of the diverse back grounds of people we all worked with every day like many people in any workplace.

This section will deal with the supervisors of the B.O.F Caster. Most of these people were once hourly workers at one point in their careers at our plant. These people for some reason were selected by management from the ranks for their abilities to represent the management side of the company. Today supervisors mainly are hired with engineering degrees and come from outside the mill. They do not have the benefits that salary people had years ago. Most of the retirement and health benefits disappear when they either lose their jobs or quit. The only area of the mill that still retains their retirement pensions and benefits is the hourly workers.

The first supervisor is Art, who came from the hourly workers in a department that shut down several years after the caster started up. He worked with my uncle Bob and stated that they shared many good times. Art was a mechanic that made salary and was transferred to the caster to use his experience in the start up and maintenance of the new caster. He went through all the training we did and also got to go to Japan to see the mills and how they worked there. He, like many of us loved to eat and also gained several pounds with all of the free food that came into the new department from outside vendors all trying to get the new orders. He was a no nonsense person that used to come up with a stern look and tell you; "Get it all done-get it all done baby". As long as you got the work done Art would let you work at your own pace and do what you wanted to. He was a good supervisor and did not push you into doing a fast job that might not be done the right way as many supervisors in the old mills did. I see him at the picnic and he is enjoying his retirement also. The next supervisor is Jim. He was a tall burly man that I worked with in the 80 inch for a short time. He would take a puff of a cigarette so hard he would smoke a third of the cigarette in one puff! He also had caster training and went to Japan. The hourly workers were supposed to go to Japan also but the extra money put aside somehow disappeared! He was in charge of the other area of the caster maintenance that built up the main pieces that made the main body of the caster. He even worked on small engines at home that were in lawnmowers, lawn trimmers, and even snow blowers. Later on he sold all the parts to one of the mechanics and received a real estate license and got into appraising homes. As the mills slowly cut benefits and perks of salary people he later left the mill and got a job as an appraiser in the real estate market. He was a good person with a heart of gold!

The next supervisor is CT he again was from Alabama and came up here because there were not many good paying jobs there. He spoke very slowly with that Southern drawl and kind of shuffled his feet when he walked. As long as you were honest and did your work he treated you very well. Some of the other workers would play jokes on him and get him mad then he would take it out on them by either giving them dirty jobs or cutting their over time back. I realized he had a difficult job and treated him with respect and we all got along good. One day we had to take a trolley wheel up to the crane and had no available mobile cranes to bring it up to the crane. CT grabbed that wheel, carried it to the elevator, then carried it the rest of the way to the crane! That wheel had to weigh at least 150

pounds! After the other workers saw this they cut way down on their practical jokes. He nominated me for an inspector job that I took. This was like a supervisor job because you had to find out why something broke and try to recommend ways to prevent breakdowns in the future! CT transferred to another department and in a slowdown was put back to an hourly worker that some had the option back then. I told CT later on to get his 30 years in, retire, then go do what he wanted to. He thanked me for the advice and that is what he did.
The next supervisor was Harry, a friend of Jim I worked in the 80 inch with. He also had a miraculous memory and could remember part numbers for all of the parts of the B.O.F.! He had a photographic mind and everyone would always come up to him for hard to find parts or spares no one could find. He originally came from the open hearth that made hot metal that the blast furnaces make today. Harry was a quiet person that talked very slow and distinctly. He would walk with his head humped down, like many of did as we got older. He had many years in the mill, I think it was over 40 years, and was one of the last of the good bosses left in the mill. He retired to his home in the country and one of his sons is one of the top law officers in his community. The last supervisor is Terry, he originally came from a salary section of the mill that set up and made spares programs for departments to organize, track, and reorder spares in the various departments. He also came from the hourly ranks as a mechanic and made salary in another department. He originally set up the spares program in the 80 inch and all over the plant. When they were completed he accepted a supervisor job in the B.O.F. in the crane and ladle metallurgical areas we worked in. He was a very good boss with a great sense of humor. He always had someone staying on overtime to cover his areas when he went home

at night. He, like many supervisors and steelworkers put in long hours in the mill. He was very smart and witty and would continually joke even in bad times. One time he went to a salary meeting and they told him to cut down on overtime. When he got out of the meeting he came down to the shop and told us what they told him. He then laughed and said, "oh by the way, who wants to work overtime tonight"! We all laughed and stayed over! Later on they had to cut salary jobs and he was one of the ones that cut was cut. He got a better job working for a brick company vendor he knew and loved the job because he did not have to work the long hours. He passed away a short time after he got this job and was missed greatly. He was one of the people that taught us that in the midst of chaos and confusion to always joke around to remove stress and keep calm!

The next section of this book will deal with the start-up of the new caster. This was the last new department that was built at the Indiana Harbor Works I worked at. With the downsizing of the steel mills and manufacturing in this country this was a rare treat to go to a brand new department. The first heat was scheduled for December, 19,1985. This was a big event and all of the maintenance staff were instructed to stay on the ground floor and not on the casting floor in case anything went wrong we would all be there to fix anything. The first heat was cast and everything went according to the plan. With that every one took a deep breath. With that we figured that there would be no mishaps. When we came to work we were all taught to look at the various stacks on the way into the mill. You could tell if both furnaces were working and if all three casting strands were operating. The day we came out for work all the stacks for the B.O.F. and caster were down! We learned that a heat was stopped because of a bad ladle gate. That opened on the

STEELWORKERS: THE LAST OF THE BREED

bottom of the ladle to let the steel out and pour it into a mold. This gate malfunctioned and instead of the ladle swinging over and pouring the steel into an emergency ladle it stopped half way poring 180 tons of steel onto casting floor and into the second floor below! It was a mess beyond belief! It was just like volcanoes you would see on TV where they burn and bury everything in their path of destruction! Everyone in the caster was assigned some form of clean-up from production to labors. Much of the new casting equipment was either buried or burned and had to be burned free with large burning torches and taken out with a mobile or overhead crane. One tool locker on the second floor was buried and half way encased in three feet of steel. All of the tools and equipment inside were burned and all of case hardened tools had to be sent out and replaced because the extreme heat of the hot steel took the hardness out of these tools and they would possibly break causing injury or damage to anyone using them. This was a plant effort with the in plant construction crews and the in department maintenance crews all working together to dig everything out, deskull; (burn the excess steel off these items), and rebuild all the damaged parts. It was a shame that all of this new equipment was destroyed but steel making is a dangerous process and accidents do happen! Also the technicians from the companies that made the caster all had to come back out for their guidance on putting this new caster back together! It again was like the caster was while it was being constructed with people and equipment all over the place! We all worked many doubles burning big chunks of steel cubes out and hauling them away to get at the buried equipment. After many weeks of work the caster was rebuilt and started up with relatively few incidents since then. Number one caster had a bad steel spill on its first start up and everyone at number two caster did everything to avoid this mistake. They even bragged that this caster would be different! It just goes to show you no matter how hard you try to prevent an accident sometimes you just cannot avoid it, that why it is called an accident!

The next section of this book will deal with extreme temperatures. I mentioned some of these temperatures in the chapter about the 80 inch and I will elaborate on these. With the good money and benefits one earns in these steel mills, there are negatives too. One of these is the terrible working conditions one has to work in. One night in the winter of 1990 we stayed over and worked a double on a wheel change on a service crane. These cranes were built in 1917 with no roller bearings and only brass bushings to act as bearings. I thought the 80 inch was bad; this was going back to the model t days! At least the 80 inch had roller bearings! The weather report that night called for cold temperatures and no one paid any attention to it. That night it got so cold that the hydraulic jack started freezing up and we had to take and put it in the crane cab heater to thaw it out. Also we took turns warming up because there were no heaters on this remote end of the building! It took twice as long as normal to change the wheel with all of the freezing up of the jack and us! That night when we got home and watched the late weather reports it was 10 degrees below zero with a wind chill of about 30 below zero! We were all glad that day was over. After that I started watching the weather reports for the days ahead and did not double on the cold or hot days, but you could not watch the weather every day so some days you just took a chance!

Another freezing experience was when one of the foremen asked us to double over cleaning up spares outside for an outside tour. The different departments had other companies and vendors that were given tours of the departments and the plant and it was the job of maintenance to clean these areas up and make them presentable to make our departments look good. Several of us agreed to stay and we were told what to do. That night it was outside using brute manpower and a fork lift tractor to move everything around and throw out unused things. That night it got cold and being pretty dark one of us got the idea to build a fire. We had extra clothes, zero caps the company issued us, and even rags wrapped around our heads to keep warm! We built a huge fire and that helped quite a lot. It also lit up the area better than it was because of the lack of light. We finished cleaning up and got home that night to find out on the news that the wind chill was 35 below! I was sick for three days after that. The next day at work we told everyone about how cold it was and that we built a huge fire to keep warm. Someone pointed out to us that thirty feet away was a main gas station. We did not know it was there at the time. They pointed out to us that if that fire would have ignited the gas station it would have killed all of us! A safety bulletin was made warning other workers of this danger and we never did that again!

I have discussed several times about the cold and now I will discuss the heat. The working conditions in these mills were one reason only the strong at heart could work in them. One night on 3/11 shift we had to go up and work on the middle crane in the 80 inch while the hot mill was running. It was summer and very hot. We went there and proceeded to do our work. After about an hour and a half I noticed all of us were just soaking wet from sweat. A little after that I noticed that I quit sweating and that I was getting shaky like I was going to pass out. One of my co-workers told me to go down and get some water. After talking to someone I found out that I had heat exhaustion! I stayed in the shop until I felt better and by that time the other workers were done with the crane. I remembered that someone before us had left a thermometer up on the crane and it read 135 degrees! This crane was in the middle of the mill building with the hot strip running below us and there was no outside air whatsoever in that area of the building! The next day the health and safety person talked to me and asked if I was alright. I told him what had happened and he told me that I had heat exhaustion. He told me either to take salt pills or when I felt faint to go and take a break. He said that when you get to the point you quit sweating and feel faint your body is slowly shutting down and that one has to drink plenty of water and rest until you feel normal. The second time I got heat exhaustion I was on the inside of the crane loosening the coupling bolts that connected the wheel to the drive shaft. I started feeling shaky and quit sweating and I told my co-workers that they had fifteen minutes to get the wheel out before I was going to go down. No one wanted the inside so they got done in a hurry and we all went down for a break. The third time I was working on the trolley of a crane while the hot coils were being rolled up and processed beneath me. I got shaky and went down for a break. The safety man was right each time I was in extreme heat I felt faint faster the second and third time. After that I was transferred to the mill and was taken off the cranes. Every time I was in a hot situation I watched myself and other workers because we had to watch over each other in that harsh environment.

    The next section will deal with the B.O.F. and the dangerous sulfur heats it makes. This sulfur is added to the furnace in the process of making steel. It is an additive that is brought down by conveyors and through a trough is added to the steel. The by product is a very deadly and dangerous gas. When this sulfur is added a warning system is activated and alarms go off on all the upper floors in the furnace area to warn everyone to evacuate the area. One day we were on the charge crane performing maintenance on the main trolley and the sirens went off. Being 80 feet in the air and 40 feet away from the furnace floor it is sometimes hard to hear. At that day we did not hear the sirens and proceeded to do our work. All of a sudden a thick cloud of dust came up to the trolley to vent out through the vents at the top of the building. Almost immediately this sulfur just takes your breath away and all of a sudden you cannot breath! It is like being suffocated! Several of us rushed to get off the trolley and get to the vents in the side of the building. It felt like we were going to pass out! After getting some air by the vents we made our way down the elevator and went outside the building for at least two hours to recuperate! It was a miracle that we did not pass out up there because we could have fallen off the trolley and that 80 foot fall would mean instant death! This was another lesson we all learned that no would go on the crane when the furnace is making any kind of heats. Our foreman had us go up there to try and save maintenance time later on in the week but it almost got us killed!

This next section will deal with the B.O.F. reline. This is a process where all the old brick is removed from the furnace and new brick is installed. When we first came to the B.O.F. in 1985 there was a reline on one of the two furnaces every six months. This process like most in these mills is a long process lasting for at least five weeks. First all of the brick is knocked out of the furnace with a huge jack hammer machine that is mobile and can be moved around. After that the furnace is tilted upside down and all of the brick is dumped out into the pit area where bucket tractors take it away. Through the years of inventing better grades of brick material and a new process of gunning material these relines were reduced from every six months to once every five years! The last reline was four years before I retired. Our supervisors told us that, for many of us, this was the last reline we will see in our careers at this plant. Installing this brick machine was a very involved process. After the brick was removed the furnace was tilted in the upright position. The brick machine was parked in between the furnaces while the furnaces were operating. Usually several weeks before the machine was used it was inspected and maintenance and lubrication was performed on it to insure it would not break down while it was being used. Then four workers climbed on top of it and hooked up four cables to an overhead lance crane and the meticulous process would begin of lifting it off its stand and bringing it to the furnace. There were huge lance hoses that had to be pulled away to guide the machine through. There was hardly any room between the lance hoses and everything else in this upper furnace area. It was like threading a needle! Once the brick machine was over the furnace it had to be set on beams that were placed there before its installation. One day when we were setting it in the lance crane bumped a beam on the furnace and it knocked down all of the accumulated dust on these beams. You could not see or move for at least fifteen minutes because it rained down nothing but black dust! It was like being in a dust storm and all you could do was just stand there! If you panicked and ran you could fall down the furnace thirty feet and would be killed or injured severely! This again was another test of one's stamina in working these mills. Once the brick machine was set in the furnace we climbed down the machine and set the base plates up on the bottom of it so the brick masons could install the new bricks from the bottom up. As they worked their way up, this platform was raised until they got to the top and all the brick was installed. Being inside the furnace you could hear every ones voice echoing like in an extinct volcano! When they were done the steps were reversed and it was put up until it was needed again. This was quite an experience to witness and to anyone who ever did this it was quite an experience!

This next section will break from the actual mill and go to a happy time of year both in the mill and all over. This is Christmas time in the mill. This time of year was a happy and thankful time of year. We all celebrated Jesus birthday by buying gifts, collecting for charities, giving money to employees who were on sick leave or to people and charities that needed help. One year we took a coat collection for the Lakota Indians in South Dakota because they did not have warm coats for the severe winters out there. One day I helped Barry, organizer of the drive, to haul the coats in my truck to a warehouse in Hammond. I helped him unload the coats on the dock and put them in linen baskets on wheels to be hauled up to the upstairs. Barry thanked me and said that it will take him several hours to haul them upstairs and put them away then call his wife to pick him up. I thought about this time of the year is to do good deeds. I told Barry, "let's all work together and get you home a lot sooner". We hauled everything upstairs and put everything away and I drove him home all in a short time. He thanked me and we both went home that night with a good feeling in our hearts.

Our mechanical shop area organized a Christmas feast for the entire B.O.F. We all brought in different food items and put them on our lunch table in the lunchroom area. Everyone agreed in a particular item. We had foods from almost every ethnic area of the world! We had Scandinavian, Mexican, Polish, German, Middle Eastern, Italian, and almost every dish you could think of. We had over three picnic tables full of food! Everyone in the B.O.F Caster complex; from management, electrical, labor, production, and everybody else came down to eat. There was so much food that people ate for several days! We all stuffed ourselves and were thanked by many for our giving. We all agreed that this was the time of year for giving! This then was a typical holiday in the steel mill.

This section will go back to the actual mill and will deal with the casting machine. The casting machine took molten hot liquid steel and when poured into a mold formed a rectangular shaped slab. This slab had an outer covering of hard steel and the inside was still liquid steel. Sometimes a leak would occur on this outer skin and the liquid steel would leak out of the slab causing what we called a "break out". This steel would leak out and would cause major damage to all the equipment. This did not happen too often but when it did it would cause a major interruption in steel making because the caster had to be shut down and all of the steel had to be burned out with torches. Then the damaged segments, parts of the caster, had to be changed for rebuilt new ones. The first ten years of the caster it ran leaded heats. These were steel with lead injected into the steel as it was poured into the caster. Then these heats were cast into leaded blooms that were sold and had an excellent ability to be machined at a processing plant. Every ladle that went through the caster completely would yield the company one million dollars! After Inland was bought by Mittal he moved this operation to another plant in the world because this process was highly toxic! After the steel went through the caster it was cut into large nine inch thick slabs with a natural gas set of automated cutting torches and sent to the 80 inch to be rolled into a steel coil for an automotive or appliance company. This casting machine was a amazing device that converted liquid steel into a solid product!

This next section will deal with the number two coke plant fire, which was just west of the B.O.F. The coke plant took coal, cooked it in a oven, then pushed it out and this made coke. Coke is used to make steel. This process is very filthy and produces very heavy toxic waste. The coke plant next to the B.O.F. produced smells that would be horrendous. They would clog up the sinuses and make one's eyes water for a long time. This plant also was a mini refinery reclaiming the byproducts and either used them in the mill or sold them. They piped the coke oven gas in pipe lines to the blooming mill and other departments to use in their furnaces. They also recovered lime that was sold to fertilizer companies. They also recovered other products that were sold to other companies making it a profitable business. With the creation of the E.P.A. and other watch dog groups these plants, like steel mills became the target of pollution alerts all over the country. Most of these old coke plants were torn down and new more energy efficient less polluting plants were built in the United States or other third world countries and the coke shipped to this country. It did not make any sense making this coke in another country and polluting there because the upper atmosphere takes this pollution and carries it all over the world dumping it on clean and dirty polluting countries all over the world! The United States and other countries closed up dirty factories here and built these factories in China and other countries. Then people wonder why we have global warming all over the world!

The coke plant fire that occurred in the late 90's was right next to the B.O.F. One morning we herd a lot of yelling outside and went to investigate. There we saw a huge fire next to one of the chemical tanks. There were many people from our department out there watching it. The fire burned for a while then it seemed to flare up and start burning even hotter than before. You could feel the heat from the fire even several hundred feet away! I had a camera from an inspector job I had at the time so I started taking pictures of the fire. There was a huge tank suspended in a water cushion on the outside and it was moving up and down. As the fire intensified and got hotter the tank would move up and down even faster. It got to the point that the tank was moving up and down so fast that water in that cushion outer ring was spewing all over the place! I got a gut feeling that this was not good. At this time there was no fire truck on the site. I asked a supervisor and he said that they called for one and that it was on its way. I talked to a coke plant worker and he told me that the tank jumping up and down contained a very toxic and highly flammable chemical in it that was why it had the outer water tank on the outer edge of it to keep it cool. He told me that if that tank jumping up and down would blow up it would destroy the whole caster, half of the B.O.F., and part of the bloomer next to the caster. Finally the fire trucks started arriving from the in plant and the nearby city fire departments. The fire was put out in a short time but the fire trucks kept putting water on the fire to cool down the metal that was heated up in the fire to prevent it from flaring up. I took several pictures of the fire, at its peak level, the floating tank, and the area after the fire. It was quite a site to see! We found out the next day that two workers were working on a valve and it exploded, killing both of them instantly, and created the fire. We also found out that the supervisor of these two men knew the valve was bad and that the upper management would not authorize to replace the valve due to budget shortfalls. The supervisor a week later felt so bad that a week later, at the site of the fire, hung himself on

STEELWORKERS: THE LAST OF THE BREED

that same valve that exploded because he felt responsible for their deaths and could not live with himself any longer. A very sad end to a bad situation! This again was a reminder to all of us what a dangerous place the steel mill was and is to work in. I told my supervisor about the pictures and he had several copies made. He was one of the last good supervisors to come up from the hourly ranks that supported the average worker. Somehow a copy made it to the union hall for the families of the killed; workers to get adequate compensation for the horrific situation that occurred.

Several years later the company built a new coke plant north of the plant and hired an outside company to come and completely tear down the old coke plant. All of the steel they tore down was re melted at our and several other mills in the area. It was strange to see these, "steel-termites", slowly cut down this complex department and reduce it down to just bare ground! It was strange to see this whole area empty where a huge bustling coke plant used to exist!

The next section will deal with our company being bought out by another company, like so many companies have been and are being bought up today even by other people from foreign countries. We went to union classes in the eighties and were shown about the global demand for steel and the amount of steel mills being built worldwide. It showed ours and several steel mills in the area in the middle of this list of mills. The mills in the middle would be the ones that would probably not survive in a severe economic slowdown. We were all depressed and just hoped we could make it at least to thirty years and get a retirement! Then several years later the mill next to us went into bankruptcy and was bought by another company. The company seemed to flourish and everyone there seemed to work unlimited over time and make lots of money. We were jealous of them at the time but did not know what was down the road. Then in 1999, Mittal bought our company and we immediately were all scared to death that we were going to have to take pay cuts or lose benefits. After hearing all the horror stories of companies bought up by other companies and the workers losing wages, benefits, and retirement accounts all terrified all of the workers in this country! Fortunately after a year we found out that everything stayed the same and if we would not have been bought out our company probably would have gone bankrupt possibly in 2003! The main thing that saved us was that the union had enough foresight to separate our retirement pension from the company in 1987 because so many companies were being bought and their pension funds stolen by these companies! What the new owner does is buy a company, streamline it, and use the assets to buy other mills. He bought mills all over the world and built an empire that was the single largest steel mill producer in the world! The mill next to us and another mill went bankrupt because of bad management. These two mills lost their pension and at a thirty year retirement were only funded at seventy-five percent by the government much like the F.D.I.C. does today for savings accounts in banks. All of us that were jealous of these two mills changed from one of envy to one of feeling sorry for these people who would have to stay and work longer because of the pension money they lost! This then was one example of many companies buying other companies, too often the worker loses, but in our case we got lucky!

The next section will deal with number ten furnace hood explosion. Ten furnace and twenty furnace are where the steel is made for the B.O.F. Ten furnace is the south furnace and closest to our mechanical shop and lunch room. This furnace, just a month ago, finished a reline of its brick lining where the

STEELWORKERS: THE LAST OF THE BREED

steel is mixed and rebuilding of its equipment related to the furnace. Above the furnace is a hood complex that takes the impurities and the gases from the furnace, cleans them in the bag house, and through flares on the top of the two hundred foot stack, burns the excess gases before it hits the atmosphere. Between the hood and the furnace is a skirt that is lowered over the furnace when the lance is lowered into the furnace so oxygen can mix the steel thoroughly. It is similar to blowing through a straw into pop in a glass when you were a child. This hood is as big as a small ranch house! It is approximately twenty three feet wide and thirty feet long. This hood has a series of water pipes welded into the outside of it for cooling purposes when mixing the hot steel over the furnace. The hood is changed when the cooling tubes become plugged up or damaged in the process of tilting the furnace. One of my jobs as an inspector was to schedule in the plant people to use their thermo graphic machines to check these tubes and make sure they have adequate water flow through them. The hood usually will last for ten years or more depending on the abuse it takes. Each furnace has this massive duct work to exit the pollution from the furnace into separate 200 foot stacks, one for each furnace. This particular hood was only a month old when one day we heard from the shop a massive explosion that rocked the B.O.F.! Everyone in the B.O.F. were; fairly used to explosions from steel being poured into the steel ladle from the furnace but this one was huge! The dust from the explosion rained down on every floor of the shop for at least fifteen minutes so you could not even go upstairs until all the dust settled. Our supervisors went upstairs first to access the damage. They found out that this furnace had a huge build up of gases in the lower hood section over the furnace and in the process that bubbles the steel (the—blow) these gases were ignited into a massive explosion that moved a hood the size of a small ranch house over one full foot! The furnace had to be shut down and the in the plant construction work force had to come in and undo the massive clamps that hold the furnace tight and move it back over to where it should be. This whole process took several weeks and many man hours due to the massive size of this hood! It was a sight to see and it reminds me, on a small scale, of building the pyramids because of all of the work it takes to change one of these units and maneuver it in place!

This last section of chapter 4 will deal with the slag pot explosion in the ladle metallurgical section of the B.O.F. This area is where the steel from the furnace area is modified to the desired specifications of the order for the caster steel. Lime or aluminum or some other element could be added to the desired order of the steel ladle. This steel is then mixed by huge electric masts that create a loud ground vibrating noise. First the ladle is brought over by a huge ladle crane and set in a de-slager cradle that tilts the ladle toward a huge scraping device that scrapes all of the slag, the debris that floats to the top of the ladle, like cream in natural milk. The scraper, de-slager, then scrapes this scum into a slag pot that is transported to the north end of the plant and is used by companies making gravel or for land fill material. This process is relatively routine and with any process in a steel mill it could turn disastrous in a second! One day my co-worker and I, and two operators were in this area doing maintenance. It was in the winter time and it felt good being near a hot ladle. Chuck was in the process of de-slaging off the slag, the other operator was by us. He and my co-worker were just getting ready to walk down the stairs. I was behind a panel board checking for any leaks. Then all of a sudden came this horrendous explosion. The fire ball came up the stairs nearly missing the two. Chuck was behind the safety glass in the small pulpit of the de-slager. I was behind the panel board. Chuck, the ladle crane man came out of his crane and down to ask us what happened. He said the fire ball came all the way to the glass operator cab of his crane. Then it went for at least 150 feet to the west all the way towards an open door. It ignited small rags and paper on the surrounding ground around the de-slager. It looked like the site after a bomb went off in a war movie! Chuck was behind the glass cab. The glass was completely cracked all over. When he used it later on in the day all the glass just fell apart! He was so shook up he had to go to the bathroom and change his clothes! We found out that being winter with the mills cutting back on people for years that they used to have a person inspect the incoming slag pots for snow or ice because the hot steel will explode if there is any ice or liquid under hot steel. This slag pot had snow and ice in the bottom and created a huge explosion when the hot steel was poured over it! Then again it was a miracle no one was hurt or killed. The crane man said that fireball was just like in a disaster movie coming right at his crane cab. Several times in these mills people were killed but there were many instances that could have been disastrous but people were spared. It was like God knew the suffering in these terrible working conditions and He looked over on us so no one would get killed or hurt. But some He could not save.

This then concludes the chapter on the 2 B.O.F. 2 Caster complex. I have dealt with the main topics I thought were the main areas of this complex department. I could have gone into detail more in other areas but I hope I touched on the main areas and topics of this and other departments.

Chapter 5
Fatalities and Injuries

    This chapter will deal with the unpleasant task of listing the fatalities and injuries in the mill from only my 32 years of working in there, to the best of my knowledge. I am listing this to show that the mills can be a happy place or a very dangerous place to work in. It is like being in combat in the military and you are on a mission in a war zone. You always have to keep your guard up and never forget that you are in a dangerous place. Once you let your guard down and become too relaxed that is when something bad happens.

    The first fatality was at the 80 Inch Hot Strip on a midnight shift. A production worker was cutting off the excess "tail' off of a steel coil. This is the steel that unwraps from a coil and drags behind it, like a ball of yarn that unravels off the ball. He was cutting this excess steel off with a torch while the hot mill crane, No. 44 crane held it in place with a huge C-hook. This was called a C-hook because it resembled a large C and is used to pick up steel coils and move them around. The brake on the hoist on the crane was not adjusted correctly and the C-hook drifted down while the man was cutting off the excess. Also the safety latch on the lower block of the crane was missing and it let the hook slip out of the C-hook. He did not see this happening because he had on burning goggles at the time. When the hook slipped out the C-hook came down on his body in the middle crushing him to death! The irony of this terrible accident was that this man had only three months to go to retire! The crane man was so shocked he had to be physically removed from the crane itself! This was a tragic story that could have been prevented with better maintenance!

The next fatality was in the 2 B.O.F. department. Primary production is where the steel is made and any time you deal with hot molten steel it is very dangerous! One day a crane machinist was doing maintenance on the north bridge of 2 Service Crane and walked on a piece of grating that was knocked loose by an explosion on the furnace earlier in the shift. Grating is thick metal that you can see through and is open to let you see through it and to let any smoke or gases in the area to pass through it and not trap anything in to create an explosion or poisoning . As he walked on this grating it gave way and he feel forty feet and landed on a spare reduction that killed him. He died in front of a fellow co-worker I worked in the crane gang with. He left three children and a wife behind. After this accident we always would repair loose grating on cranes or any walkways. It is a shame that all too often someone will have to die or be injured to do maintenance or put up warning lights like at a train crossing in everyday life!

The next fatality occurred at a pit outside the B.O.F. lunch room. It is a pit that traps debris in and when it becomes plugged up it had to be cleaned out. This particular time a worker went into the pit to start vacuuming out the sludge with a huge suction hose. The pit was not tested for any gases before the person entered the pit. These pits, especially in primary production collect gases that linger in these areas because there is no air circulation to move them out. This person went down a ladder and became consumed by the gases and passed out. His coworker saw him and rushed down the ladder to help him. He too passed out and a third worker went down the ladder to help. All three of these workers in a chain reaction were killed by poisonous gases! After this accident it was brought up in monthly safety meetings that everyone had to first test any area that was a confined space for poisonous gases, the worker had to put on an oxygen tank gas mask, and if that worker would pass out the other workers could not go into the pit unless they had on the proper oxygen tank and mask!

The next injury deals with an electrician, Gil, that was involved in an upper limit cable change on the charge crane. This crane charges the steel into the furnaces that is why it is called the charge crane. It was a simple limit cable change. The upper limit prevents the crane block from going up all the way underneath the trolley and breaking the cable and falling down. This upper limit is simply an arm that goes up and down with a hanging weight on it suspended by a cable. An electrician cleans the limit mechanism when this cable is changed. Gil was about to clean this when something happened and the cable became tangled up on the limit and the arm struck him on the knee and leg. It was so severe that it broke his leg and dislocated his knee! He had to be carried off the crane and taken to the hospital for treatment. He was off work for almost a year. He had to undergo extensive therapy before he could go back to work. He, like many who have been injured, were paid compensation for their injuries, either by the companies that made these inferior products, or the main company we all worked for. Still, himself like all the others who have been injured; would gladly give back this money to reverse the damage they suffered in these injuries! Gil returned to work and put in 44 years of service until he retired about when I did!

The next is a fatality at the 2 B.O.F. in the hot metal section. This is where hot metal is brought in from the blast furnace to be mixed in the B.O.F. This occurred after I retired so the exact details I do not know about. It was a metal handrail that was broken by the crane hitting it and the operator leaned on it to look into the pit area. As he leaned on this rail it gave way and he fell onto a car that moves the ladles and was knocked out. No one was around and the car moved crushing him to death. He was a labor that transferred into production and was alone on the job because of the mills and many jobs today with only the minimum amount of workers to make a product!

The next fatality is at the #3 Cold Strip Mill. This mill takes a coil of steel and processes it into a more refined flat steel. It can be rerolled to a thinner thickness, it's sides cut shorter, or heat treated to make it stronger. Every so many years the sheet metal on the roofs on these buildings, like anything, has to be replaced. These workers were an in the plant department with our company that replaced the corrugated sheeting that was rusted out from years of harsh mill chemicals and Midwest winters. These workers always wear a safety life line similar to a mountain climber. For some reason that day one of the workers took off his safety line. He walked over to a section of rusted roof and it gave way. He fell down about sixty feet to his death! It was a shame that for only a little bit he took off his safety belt but some times that is all it takes!

The next is an injury at the old #2 coke plant. This person was my brother-in-laws neighbor in the old subdivision we all lived in at the time. He only had a right arm and was missing his left arm. He told me the story one day when we were out fishing. He was working at the coke plant in a little warehouse with an open door next to a set of railroad tracks. Something happened in the warehouse that knocked him out and in the process he landed on the train rails outside of the building. When he woke up he was in excruciating pain because his left arm was cut off from the wheels of a passing train. He spent a long time in rehab and recovered well. The company gave him a life time job as it did when workers were injured in the mill. He worked all over the mill and retired with 38 years of service. I still see him at the picnics and other places and he is enjoying retirement like most of us.

Next is the three fatalities, previously mentioned, that died in the #2 coke plant explosion and fire that killed two workers. The third worker died one week later from hanging himself due to the guilt of blaming himself for the deaths of the other two workers over a faulty valve that was not changed.

Next; is the fatalities at #4 B.O.F. This department was similar to our department only it had larger furnaces and a strainer system that cleaned the molten steel of impurities. #4 B.O.F. , like many departments, had a mobile work force assigned to it to fill in for vacations or extra jobs that needed extra workers. One day about five of these workers, we called them, "bull-gang", were to burn up and carry out the pieces of an old pipe line going through a conveyor system that carried coke up to the bins of the B.O.F. to be used in the furnace. They began burning on what they thought was an abandoned line and a huge explosion erupted that could be heard almost all over the plant! Then all we could hear was several sirens rushing to the B.O.F. We found out later that these workers mistakenly used a gas torch and burned into the wrong line! They burned into a live oxygen line and it exploded killing two workers immediately and sparing three workers that were not directly in the path of the explosion. The steel mills are very dirty places to work in and the primary production areas everything is black. All of the pipes in this area were not labeled lines and they burned on the wrong line causing the massive explosion! After this accident there was considerable attention to washing and labeling all of the combustible lines in the plant, especially primary production areas. It is a shame that some one always has to die to get attention to safety! It is like many people have to get killed at a train crossing before they install gates and warning lights!

The next injury occurred at #7 Blast Furnace; one of the largest blast furnaces in North America and built in 1980. A production worker was doing a routine job near a pit area where the molten steel accumulates. It is like a holding area. He was on the edge of this pit when all of a sudden he lost his balance and feel into the hot pit! His instant reaction was to climb out and in doing this burned his one leg so bad it had to be amputated! He survived but had to go on disability the rest of his life because of the burns. Just for a couple of seconds the molten hot steel burned his leg almost to the bone!

This plant has been in existence for over one hundred years and has many stories and folklore incidents. The original plant was in what they call plant 1. To the north, northwest, and northeast are all landfill areas. The byproducts of making steel are slag and molten ash and were dumped into the lake to fill in areas for future departments. The company had no use for these waste products and could dump them into the lake back then. Then the E.P.A. got involved in the 1970's and stopped the dumping. Then the company processed this waste and sold it to outside companies for different uses. This landfill amounted to a vast amount of new land! People told me stories of fishing right off the back of the 44 hot strip mill directly into the lake! This landfill accounted for miles of extra land where these departments were built on: plant 3 coke plant, plant 2 coke plant, one to six blast furnaces, 2 open hearth, 2 B.O.F., 2 caster, 2 bloomer, 10-12 inch bar mill, main roll shop, 1&2 cold strip mills, 76 inch hot strip mill, 80 inch hot strip mill, 4 B.O.F., 1 caster, 7 blast furnace, 3 cold strip mill, the main trucking garage, the main stores plant, and many more departments. This huge landfill amounted to the creation of most of the plant that is there today at the Harbor Works Plant I worked in!

With this additional landfill comes many stories of large dump trucks backing up to the lake and toppling into the lake with the driver either being killed or never finding his body. There were old pictures years ago in libraries of trucks and other equipment going into the lake. I know for fact that in the 1980's a huge iron ore crane bridge toppled over in a storm in plant one. We saw the several hundred foot span crane bridge after it was blown over. It took a long time to repair and put it back in service, the crane man was lucky he was not killed!

There was even a story of some mechanics at 7 blast furnace making a ramp and setting large oxygen tanks on this ramp, then knocking off with a hammer the valves and shooting them out into the lake! Supposedly they were either fired or reprimanded severely because of the extreme danger of knocking off a valve on a highly pressurized tank and propelling it out into the air several hundred feet!

There is also a story about a bad train wreck that happened either in the Harbor near the plant or in the plant that possibly involved someone or something important. Somehow this train was taken to the plant one, the original site of the plant, and put into a small building and sealed up and has never been opened again. We were at the old round house, that is where they used to turn trains around to go the opposite way, one day we were looking for spares and one of my co workers told me that story. You could see the building and a huge lock on the door and evidence that it has not been opened in years!

Another story, from plant one again, was about a worker that fell into a pit in number one open hearth. He was killed and the billet that contained his body was taken out and buried some place in plant one with a plaque on stating his name and department he died in. No one I knew of knew where the plaque was but that it did exist somewhere!

There were, and I am sure today, there are many injuries that are caused by slipping or tripping over things. Many of the steel workers are getting older, like myself and a lot of us, and the body just does not bend or the eyes cannot see things like we did when we were younger. Today in the mills there are a rare occurrence happening because there are the older workers and the younger workers recently hired in to replace workers retiring. There are no workers in the middle in the seniority ladder, like there was when I worked there! Also there are much fewer workers in the workplace today so that means that workers have to do more work. The worker that had someone to look out for him is not there today. The mills and factories today operate with a fraction of the workers they had years ago putting more of the work load on the workers and in turn causing more injuries as the inexperienced young worker and the older worker try to do the same or more with less.

These then are the injuries, fatalities, and stories that I have heard in my 32 years working at the plant. The fatalities and injuries are true. The landfills are true, but the train wreck and the billet are rumors and no one knows for sure.

Chapter 6
Departments that Closed

This chapter will consist of the departments that closed down in my 32 years at the mill. Sadly enough this time period is when the mills started closing down inefficient or non profitable departments. These departments made a range of steel products from rail spikes to tin for soup cans. The company's belief, years ago was to make a wide variety of steel products and to diversify widely to protect its profitability in good as well as bad times. Also my company was known for its individual orders of making a small order for many customers. The other mills around the area only wanted to take the big orders only for customers. These mills would run large orders and not have to reset their mills for days unlike our company that would run three runs then have to reset their mills for another small order. This practice of catering to the small customer kept our company working steady in the lean times while the big order mills would be idle. Then with the election of a new president in the eighties and a severe downsizing of American steel and manufacturing jobs these companies seemed to catch a disease. The mentality of giving an American a good paying job for a good days work seemed to end. These companies went on a rampage of cost cutting and downsizing. The idea of making several steel items faded and these mills shrank down to producing slabs and coils that were for the automotive and appliance industry with a few other departments making select bar and shape products. This chapter will list the departments and the approximate year they closed down. The mill I worked at there are still many buildings there but only about one third of them are functioning departments as with the steel mills that are left in this country.

The first department was #1 Open Hearth located in plant one. There they made the steel that was poured into ingots, large rectangular solid steel cubes, that were sent to a department, reheated, then rolled out into a plate or coiled steel coil. This department was built probably in the early nineteen hundreds for the plate steel that was produced near it in the 100 Inch Plate Mill. This department was shut down with the start up of #1 Caster in approximately 1973. The Round house was in this area and was like a huge wagon wheel that would turn on rollers and turn trains around to go in the opposite direction. Also these trains could be worked on and serviced in this huge building. With the downsizing of Plant 1 in the early seventies these areas were closed down because the expansion was in the northern part of the plant.

Plant 3 Coke Plant was located between plant 4 and plant2 near A&B Blast Furnaces. This plant was built possibly in the early seventies for #2 & #3 open hearth for raw coke production and the new #4 B.O.F., at the time. What we heard was that an outside company built it cheaply and it was plagued with problems from the start. It finally shut down after a short time and was years later torn down.

The next department is A & B Blast Furnaces. These were built for World War II for the bar mills that, were located in Plant 4. With their downsizing and less demand for open hearth metal they were closed down in approximately 1980. It was found out later on that Inland should have kept these going because they had shortages of hot metal in the plant, but by then the department was idled too long and the company had to buy hot metal from other mills. One interesting note, there was a gangster movie set in the 1930's, made in the 80's staring Paul Newman and one of the background scenes of the movie was the A & B Blast Furnaces located off of Dickey Road in Indiana Harbor! The scene made the front page of our in the plant newspaper we used to have and it was exciting to see Hollywood come to the steel mills!

The next department that shut down was a partial shut down. Years ago there were six small blast furnaces located just west of our #2 Coke Plant. These were small and were built to provide hot metal for #2 & #3 Open Hearth at the time. With the conversion to #2 B.O.F., from #2 Open Hearth there was no longer a need for that much metal and four of the six furnaces were shut down in approximately 1980. These furnaces were partially torn down then left open to air out for several years before being torn down completely. Only numbers five and six furnaces were left and I think are still in operation today. Plus the building of #7 Blast Furnace this huge furnace supplied all the hot metal for #4 & #2 B.O.F.'s.

The next department was #3 Bloomer located near the 44 Hot Strip. This department made blooms out of ingots for the structural mills and the 10 & 14 Inch mills that were near it. With less demand for blooms this department shut down in approximately 1985. One day we had to go over and get some spare lockers from this and other shut down departments. It is an eerie feeling to go in these shut down departments and hear the silence. It is like you can still hear these mills going and people talking and laughing during their work day! It feels like these areas are haunted and you can sense someone or something is near you!

The forge department was a small shop located in the old plant 1 area and made rail spikes for the railroad rails, pinch bars, chisels, and large tools that were forged out bar steel and made in the plant. With the downsizing in the 80's this department was closed in about 1985. Then these tools were purchased from an outside vendor from then on. The supervisors told us that it was cheaper buying these tools from the outside because they did not have to pay for the wages and benefits of these workers that made these things. This was another sign of the downsizing of the American manufacturing jobs. The issue of wages and benefits that took decades and a lot of blood, sweat and tears to gain were slowly being eliminated. When these businessmen talk of a world economy, what they really mean, is that industrialized countries like the United States and Great Brittan wages have to be lowered to meet an underdeveloped country wages. This process destroys our manufacturing middle class as it has in the developed industrialized countries in the world!

The next department is the 44 Hot Strip Mill. This department was built in the late 1930's as the country was painstakingly coming out of the Great Depression and Hitler was invading Europe. The demand for sheet steel was increasing and Inland only had a plate mill so it had to build a hot strip mill. The 44 mill was the premier mill for many years. It ran full steam during WWII then continued after that in the retooling stage after the war. It was the only hot strip mill so it was the most sought after department to work in the entire plant. There were many stories of workers backstabbing each other and turning other people in to the bosses to get special favors or overtime. There were also stories of rollers on the finishing mills and production people making huge sums of money with the tonnage incentive scales that were in place then. My father-in-law got a job there after the war in metallurgy and did well there as many workers did. Some people from the 44 transferred to the 80 Inch mill and told us many stories of the glory days of the 44! When this mill shut down as the new #2 Caster started up in 1985 we had to go over there one night for caster spares we had stored there. It was an eerie sight to see a once busy department just setting there idle. You could see the date of the last strip that was rolled on the mill written on a production chalk board on the main mill. I had to run the mill crane and could not find the switch to turn it on. I had to go find an electrician and he showed me a hidden button you could only see if you moved your head all the way to the left of the crane cab! I told him that this mill with their hidden secrets still lives on and he agreed. The workers would write procedures or the right way to build something and keep it in their special books only they had to make sure their good jobs were safe! Many secrets existed in this mill and some of the people that transferred to the 80 Inch took this mentality with them! The workers had social building classes where the mentality of the old days of hiding information were out of date and the workers were encouraged to all work together for the good of each other. This mentality took several years to change and it did help people to work together more than they did.

    The next department that closed up was the #1 & 2 Cold

STEELWORKERS: THE LAST OF THE BREED

    Strip Mill. This department was, from working with people that used to work there, employed around a thousand people in its " heyday" in the 1950's till the early eighties. There they processed steel coils from the 44 and 76 mills and made tin for the can industry. Then in the eighties, with the downsizing of steel, they slowly began to shrink. In the late eighties they finally closed down with the exception of a tiny coiling line employing only about five people! Our department, like other departments, started using these closed departments to store their spare parts. In the early nineties our department began storing spares there. We were assigned the job of moving several thousand old motors and old spares out of one area to be used for our spare parts for our department. Other departments also stored their parts in this and other shut down departments to keep these spares out of the harsh weather. Most of the old equipment was sold to South America, China, and U. S. Steel and was removed from these areas leaving a vast area of storage potential. The mobile work force, the "Bull Gang", hose rebuilding, engineering, and several departments stored their spares there. It was again a shame to see a huge department bustling department close down to a ghost town situation!

    #11 Coke Battery was built the same time that #7 Blast Furnace was built and started up in 1980. This coke battery supplied coke for the production of hot metal for the b. o. f. 's in the plant. This coke plant, like No. 3 in plant 3, was plagued with problems from the start! The same people that built plant 3 built #11 and you think that management would learn from their past mistakes but they did not and this turned out to be a disaster and closed down in approximately 1989! With all of these departments closing down, the workers that could bid to transfer to other departments and I worked with several workers that came from there. They said that this department was built very cheaply with inferior materials and was managed very badly by people that did not know what they were doing! It was a shame that this department, like the other coke plant, did not last long! Some of these workers were laid off and told that they probably would never be called back again. Some were even laid off for three to five years then eventually all of the laid off workers for all of the steel mills in the area were called back to work as steel orders eventually picked up and people retired!

The next department that closed down was the 100 Inch Plate Mill. This mill was built at the beginning of the 1900's and was the only rope driven mill left in the United States! The drive unit had a large flywheel that was driven by a motor that was connected to a large flywheel by a series of approximately 1 ¼ inch ropes. These ropes were connected together by a process called "marrying" or joining the ropes together. The riggers from the rigging department were the only ones that knew how to do this job. Sadly the company gradually phased out the rigging department through retirements and these people's skills are also not used today in the steel mills. The plate mill was Inland's first mill that made flat steel and was used to make floor plate. If you ever walked on board a ship or steel floor and it had dimples in it that was probably floor plate. They also used floor plate in the building of ships and many other uses. With this process a steel slab was heated up in a furnace and "back-passed" or ran back and forth in a mill stand until the desired length and thickness is required. The mill stand rolls had dimples imbedded into them from a roll shop and these dimples created the dimples into the flat plate steel. When the new caster started up several of these employees, including a person I went to high school with and have not seen in years, transferred out of this department because of the rumors of it closing down. Then in 1989 this department, like many others, closed its doors for good. The flywheel from this "dinosaur" department ended up in the Smithsonian Institution out East as a national heirloom!

The next department that closed down was the 76 Inch Hot Strip Mill that was located right next to the 80 Inch. This department was built approximately at or after World War II. It was built for larger width and larger coils of steel needed then for demand. It was a larger mill than the 44 Hot Strip and supplied the auto and appliance industry for the large demand for goods after World War II. This mill was the main mill in the plant for many years until the 80 was built in 1965. The 80 Inch was a larger mill and made the steel much faster than the 76 mill. I also found out that my uncle Bob worked there for 44 years until he retired! This mill along with the downsizing was closed down in approximately 1991 leaving only the 80 Inch as the only hot strip mill left in the company!

The next department was #2 Bloomer which made long slender rectangular shapes of metal from large billets that were rolled out and used in the structural areas of the mill. Blooms were turned into I-beams, h-beams, angles, channels, flats, rail road rails, and other structural shapes. If Inland did not make these shapes these blooms were sold to other mills that processed them and made the necessary shapes out of them for the market. Departments, that used the structural steel, were the 10 & 14 Inch and the Electric Furnace structural department. Also several workers transferred to the caster because of rumors of this department closing down. Then in approximately 1991 this department also closed down as the company continued a slow process of getting out of the structural steel market and to concentrate on the flat rolled market that supplied the auto and appliance market.

The next department that closed made every worker and the E.P.A. happy it was #2 Coke Plant. This was the department you could smell of toxic benzene before you even got near it. After the bad fire and costly government fines and complaints from everybody on the working conditions it finally closed up in approximately 1991 also. This department was so toxic that six months later we went looking for spares in and for a couple of hours exposure our sinuses were plugged up for several days! Inland for several years bought coke from other mills until with a joint venture with other companies built a new coke plant in the northern part of the plant north of our department. This old coke plant was just too costly to maintain. This department was let set and air out for at least five years before an outside company came in to tear it down. This was quite a process to see of the metal crunching cranes and tractors taking the metal and cutting this steel like it was nothing. I called these machines "steel-termites" because of the way they cut and chewed up the steel beams and pipes like they were straw! This outside company tore down the department for free and sold the steel it reclaimed to ours and other steel mills. That seemed a strange agreement but that is the way they did it back then. It took about a year to tear the whole department down to the bare ground. It was an area the size of several city blocks and it seemed strange to see all of this bare land when we were used to seeing buildings and pipes! We used to kid ourselves that some day , the way they were closing these departments and other than the toxic waste, this land is prime land on the lake and would be a great place for an amusement park! This is why I am listing all of these departments because if you drive by this and other mills they still look huge. The reality is that two thirds to three fourths of these buildings are empty inside. The insides of these mills have been gutted and these buildings are used for parking of vehicles, storage of parts, or just empty!

The next department that closed down was the last open hearth at the plant, No. 3 Open Hearth. This department stayed in production because of its ability to make specialty steel that was needed for a particular order. I never worked in an open hearth, but working with people that have worked there, it is the combination of a blast furnace and B.O.F. that produces a unique blend of steel that is poured into an ingot and is later converted into a slab or bloom to be used in coil steel or structural steel. As far as I know this open hearth was the last one left in America! These were replaced and all shut down by 1991.

The next department was called #4 Slaber, which made slab steel for the 44, 76, and 80 inch hot strips. As these other departments closed down the 80 inch was the only department left to use this steel. With the plant going to all cast steel in 1985 there was no demand for ingot into slabs. The slaber kept going for several years because it made special orders and was sold to other companies and was shut down completely in 1991. This department took an ingot, heated it up, and back-passed this red hot ingot back and forth in one four roll mill stand until it got to the shape of a bloom or slab of steel. This method was alright in the old days but exposed the steel to air and rusted faster. The cast steel is less exposed to air and has a much better quality of steel for the automotive and appliance industry.

The next department that closed kept a few people working there but the actual department shut down. The Mold Foundry used to set up huge molds which slag pots and other large vessels were poured into creating a cast product. These large slag pots were used in the mill to carry scrap liquid steel or slag, this product is at the top of a steel ladle something like cream in milk. They also carried another form of slag, this was like powdered dirt but it was steel. If the B.O.F. had a ladle that could not go through the caster and for some reason could not be returned to the furnace this ladle was poured into a mold of a slag pot so that the steel would not be wasted. The mold yard made many vessels out of steel that could not be recycled back into steel production. One funny thing, the department shut down but kept a few men working there that went to these departments to set them up to use recycled steel in the form of slag pots and other vessels to be used in the mill.

The 10 & 14 Inch Mills were located next to the #2 Bloomer and rolled out the blooms into structural shapes of angles, I-beams, H-beams, or square stock used in the structural building areas of the construction industry. This mill was about a half mile long and again in its heyday was filled with workers and mills churning out all types of steel. Going through these shut down quiet stripped out departments one can almost hear the ghosts of the past yelling out, "hey watch out, here comes another load so put it on the train car to be sent out"! These departments all have stories and one for the 10 & 14 mill was that a labor was hired to work there. He did not know what to do and everyone was too busy to break him in on a job. So he got a piece of chain and dragged it all the way down to the other end of the department and then sat down and took a break. After he rested he dragged it to the other end and did the same thing. After weeks of doing this someone watched him and asked him what he was doing. He told them the story about how no one had time to show him what to do. The man just laughed and saw his boss and got

STEELWORKERS: THE LAST OF THE BREED

him a job doing real work. There is another story, in this mill, about someone that was stealing lunches from the refrigerator. One of the workers played a trick and put "cretin-oil" on a sandwich. This is some type of strong laxative. The worker would see who was stealing all the food from the refrigerator. The next day he saw a man rushing down the mill floor as fast as he could go to the bathroom! He watched him for two days doing this and was sick and weak on the job! He then told all of his worker friends about this event and that stopped the lunch stealing!

The next area to close was the personnel office. It was originally located in Plant 1 next to the clinic and was relocated to an old refinery office then to an office located in a closed down tank manufacturing plant. With the purchase of the company and the closing in of jobs in the steel industry the personnel office was closed down in 2001 and was moved to an outside company for hiring of new employees. This was another move of the once family oriented company to a more performance based company. But, I might add, that current employees could recommend new hires and this did help some one to be hired by the company. It was just the personal ties to a particular Human Resource person was eliminated.

The next area to close was the company newspaper, the Steelmaker. This newspaper had been around for many decades, the exact time it was created I do not know. With the new company focusing more on the internet this icon of our company was closed down in about 2002. It was another sign of the changing times of our world. The paper was always at the clock houses or delivered to our departments and had every thing from in the plant news to the want add section.

The final department, I know of, to close was the Rigging Department. This department changed all of the cables on all of the cranes in the entire plant! This was a lot of cranes back when all of these departments were operating! This group of people, were trained how to weave rope together and how to blend new cables into the old gradually replacing the old cables until only the new ones remained. I might add that they did start one new department in approximately 1999 and it was called the crane-gang. This was a central department that took care of all of the cranes in the plant. The rigging aspect of changing cables and all of the crane work went to this department. Half of the remaining riggers went into this group. The few remaining, maybe a handful stayed in the rigging department, mainly just cable inspectors, until they all retired in approximately 2005 then this department was also officially closed for good.

The other service departments that serviced the mills either closed down or cut back on their employees. These departments, then again I am not sure of all of them, were the track gang, carpenter shop, field forces, mold foundry, and other departments that I do not know of.

This section is then the listing of the departments that closed down in my 32 years that I worked at the former Inland Steel Company. I listed these departments for a reason, to show the reader the magnitude of the number of people that this mill cut down on in just the 32 years I worked in this plant! This is only one plant in the United States, multiply this times the hundreds of plants that have closed down in this country and the numbers are astounding! The next chapter will list just the mills that closed down from Chicago to Burns Harbor in Indiana, the Northwest Indiana corridor in the last 30 years.

Chapter 7
Past and Present Employment in the Mills

This chapter will give the reader, to the best of my knowledge; the scope in numbers about how much this country has went from a manufacturer to a service economy. The wage scale for a factory worker used to be 15 to 25 dollars an hour, called a living wage in the year 1979. A living wage is a job an individual can get and afford to buy a house, car, and raise a family on a comfortable wage scale. In the 30 years that have passed the average job for a worker today is a service job, let us say at Wall Mart, where the average wage there is 8 dollars an hour. This is a wage cut of 7 to 17 dollars an hour! This has been a gradual reduction through our elected leaders and businessmen. Many of these factories closed down in this country only to open up in China and Mexico where there is plenty of cheap labor and no pollution laws! These leaders forgot that they shut down polluting plants in this country and moved them to cheap labor countries but the pollution from these companies is carried all over the world in the jet stream and eventually all of us suffer!

I will list these figures, but they are not exact, just to show the magnitude of the job loss just in the area of Northwest Indiana to the Chicago area from 1979 to the present. I might add that, even with this massive job loss, this area is the most concentrated area for the integrated mills in the country!

The first company was U.S. Steel, located away from the current mill in Gary, but in South Chicago. This company was an extension of the main U.S. Steel and the facilities were no longer needed. My father's neighbor, Paul, worked there and he told me that the plant, in its prime, employed at least 10,000 people in the early seventies. He said that after they closed it down it set for a couple of years to air out the pollution then an outside scrap company came in and cut it all down to the ground and sold the steel to the remaining steel mills in the area.

The next mill was called Wisconsin Steel and it also was located in South Chicago near U.S. Steel. With the winding down of Viet Nam and the closing of inefficient mills this complex was shut down, like U.S. Steel, a few departments at a time until the whole plant closed down. I remember seeing a documentary on television about how shutting down a large company affects the whole surrounding neighborhood and area businesses alike. Restaurants, bars, cleaners, repair shops, and many other businesses also closed down after all of these plants closed. It is like a huge tidal wave and just everything in its path is destroyed. This mill also was cut down for the scrap steel. This plant employed approximately 5,000 people and also went down to zero people.

The next mill is Acme Steel and is located in Illinois farther south of Chicago. I knew a man that worked there and he told me he was manager of a department there and that the entire plant, in its heyday, employed at least 5,000 people. He said

STEELWORKERS: THE LAST OF THE BREED

with the scaling back that went on that the plant today maybe has 500 people left.

The next four companies I am going to put together because each one of them in approximately 1979 employed 26,500 people. These companies are: Youngstown Sheet and Tube, Inland Steel, U.S. Steel, and Bethlehem Steel. These companies are located next to each other on the southern tip of Lake Michigan in Indiana. This would be a grand total of 106,000 people! These four companies today employ about 6,000 a piece for a total of 24,000 people.

All of these companies I have just listed employed approximately 126,000 people! The support companies that did work for these mills in the area were fabrication shops, cables for the cranes and for lifting weights, bearings, clothes, safety gear, machining equipment, tools, and many other support areas. In general, like in combat, there are ten support groups needed for every worker on the floor. This number would then be multiplied by ten for a grand total of 1,260,000 million jobs in the year of 1979! Today there are approximately 24,500 jobs and with a ten person support level only 245,000 jobs left! That is a decrease of over one million jobs in a once bustling area!

In 1979 basically one in every four people worked a manufacturing, refinery, or steel mill job in this area. You could get a job in two hours, work it, if you did not like it, quit it and get another job you liked in a couple of days. Today it will take you two years, if you are lucky, just to get one of these jobs good or bad! Basically 25% of the population in this area was a manufacturing type job. Today less than one per cent of the population has a manufacturing type job!

I have listed these numbers just to let the reader know the magnitude and scope of how much this area has changed.

This area is typical of how the whole country, in general, has changed. We have went from a nation of makers to a nation of consumers!

Conclusion

I went to our 25 year picnic last Saturday and told many people I worked with that the book I told them I was going to write is finally finished and they are eager to read it! I wrote this book because most of the books written today are famous people or politicians that cannot relate to the average person. This book is written exclusively for the average person to relate to and enjoy. It is also written to let the readers know how much of the people that made things in this country and help build this country are gone today. These people are just forgotten and every one thinks that computers and high tech will save us. We must never forget that mankind and God controls man's destiny and if we ever forget this we will not survive! In World War II our parent's generation built a back up system in the bombers to manually raise and lower the landing gears in the planes in case the hydraulics failed. This world is not building in a manual device to prevent a catastrophic landing!

So I hope you will enjoy the book and relate to it in many ways and to see what people just like you and I have and do today to keep this great country going!